LIFE AND INFLUENCE
OF THE
REV. BENJAMIN RANDALL

Benjn Randall

LIFE AND INFLUENCE

OF THE

REV. BENJAMIN RANDALL

FOUNDER OF THE

FREE BAPTIST DENOMINATION

Mr. Randall never ceased to love the larger Baptist body. In
his spirit and that of our common Master this volume is written.

By REV. FREDERICK L. WILEY

———

PHILADELPHIA

AMERICAN BAPTIST PUBLICATION SOCIETY

BOSTON   CHICAGO   ST. LOUIS
TORONTO, CAN.

TO

The Rev. Hosea Quinby, D. D.

AN EARLY EDUCATOR IN OUR HIGH-GRADE SCHOOLS,
AN ABLE MINISTER OF THE LORD'S GOSPEL,
WHO HAD IT IN PURPOSE TO PUBLISH
A BIOGRAPHY OF BENJAMIN RANDALL,
BUT WAS CALLED TO HIGHER LIFE
DURING THE INITIAL PROCESSES,
THIS WORK IS GRATEFULLY
DEDICATED

" Feeding on lives and deeds im-
mortal, we grow strong in exalted
resolve and actions divine."

FOREWORD

THE first Free Baptist church I ever saw soon became my religious home; and membership in the body of Christians that church represented has been continuous to the present time, during more than sixty years. Mine was a case of "falling in love at first sight." But, like all properly placed affection, that love has deepened and strengthened with the passing years.

While yet in the days of my youth, I began to investigate the conditions that were claimed in justification of our existence as a separate religious body. That interested me in the founder of this body, Benjamin Randall. As I studied the character, labors, and usefulness of this man, I was thrilled with an inexpressible admiration for him.

I eagerly devoured all available printed literature about Mr. Randall and his times.

Foreword

I visited New Durham, the place of his residence during his ministry, while yet unpublished facts and authentic traditions about him were fresh in the memory of the oldest people of the locality. Some of these were questioned. I had access to records written by Mr. Randall, which, if published, would make two or three respectable volumes. These were laid under tribute.

The Rev. Hosea Quinby, D. D., had it in his heart to publish a biography of Benjamin Randall; but, in 1878, died with only a mass of scrappy material to represent his purpose. This was placed in my hands for discretionary use. A careful reading of this collection discovered but few facts usable for this work that I had not already gleaned from other sources. Some of these facts have been assimilated.

Up to this stage of my search for facts respecting Mr. Randall, some of my experiences—though lacking in some points of analogy—have reminded me of Carlyle's quest for Cromwell. For more than two

Foreword

hundred years, facts about the religious life and wise statesmanship of Oliver Cromwell were buried in comparative obscurity. " Thomas Carlyle, with his passion for men who have done something, divined the truth about Cromwell, even before he began his search among the rubbish-heaps of papers and pamphlets relating to his period of the commonwealth, which had been dumped in a confused mass in the British Museum."

Among the books that have been helpful for reference, especially in writing the section on " Posthumous Influence," grateful mention would be made of the " Life of Benjamin Randall," by Rev. John Buzzell; " History of the Freewill Baptists," by Isaac D. Stewart, D. D.; " Centennial Record," by the Free Baptist Printing Establishment; the " Free Baptist Cyclopedia," by Rev. G. A. Burgess, A. M., and John T. Ward, D. D.; " Missionary Reminiscences," by Mrs. M. M. H. Hills; and the " History of the Free Baptist Woman's Missionary Society," by Mrs. Mary A. Davis.

Foreword

As all of these works are now out of print, it seems fitting that a brief biography of Benjamin Randall and a summary of his posthumous influence be given to the current public. "Men who have understanding of the times, to know what Israel ought to do," have conceded the demand for such a work. To have the assurance of the same men that the humble manuscript submitted holds the supply of this demand is very gratifying to the writer.

If the finished product shall to any extent serve as an interpreter of Benjamin Randall and our people to the world—if to any extent it shall strengthen the bond of union between our people and the larger Baptist body, so that the relation, now sympathetic and cooperative, may, in the near future, become organic—these results will be in line with the desire, prayer, and hope of the author.

FREDERICK L. WILEY.

LACONIA, N. H., October, 1914.

CONTENTS

PART I

THE LIFE-STORY

Contents

Contents

Contents

PART II
POSTHUMOUS INFLUENCE

LIST OF ILLUSTRATIONS

PART I

THE LIFE-STORY

B

I

ANCESTRY AND EARLY YEARS
1749-1770

A S with the heavenly bodies, so with some earthly bodies, in contemplation of them, we may "think God's thoughts after him." As with the heavenly bodies, so with Benjamin Randall. In his sterling ancestry, his eventful career, and his glorious ascension to the life more abundant, we have a clear illustration of the design, the providence, and the grace of God.

New Castle, New Hampshire, is the place where Benjamin Randall first saw the light of this world. New Castle is a rock-bound island, with an area of about seven hundred acres. It is so near Portsmouth as to be connected to the city by a bridge, and yet is mostly open to the broad ocean. It has deep-water surroundings, thus allowing the easy and safe approach of the largest craft. In

[3]

Benjamin Randall

the early times New Castle, then called Great Island, held the highest rank in the colony. Its position attracted settlers as early as 1623. This island was for years not only the general mart of business for the infant colony, but the residence of the colonial governors and other leading men, the place where courts were held and justice dispensed.

William Randall, born about 1610, is the only immigrant to America by the name of Randall of whom we have any knowledge. He came to Rhode Island in 1636, but was at Marshfield, Massachusetts, in 1637. In 1640 we find him settled in Scituate, Massachusetts, where, by his wife Elizabeth, he had Sarah, born in 1640; Joseph, March, 1642; Hannah, March, 1644; William, December, 1647; John, April, 1650; and Benjamin, 1659.

Joseph Randall, second, married, in 1673, Hannah, daughter of William Macumber, and had Elizabeth and Sarah, twins, born in 1673; Joseph, 1675; Hannah, 1677;

[4]

Benjamin Randall

Sarah, 1680; Margaret, 1683; Mary, 1684; and Benjamin, 1688.

The last named, Benjamin Randall, married Mary, daughter of Hon. Shadrach Walton, of New Castle, New Hampshire, where he settled. Respecting the children of this pair we know nothing, except that one was a son, who was also named Benjamin. This son Benjamin was born about 1712, and married Margaret, daughter of Capt. Benjamin Mordantt, sometimes called Mordan. This Benjamin Randall of 1712 was known as Captain Randall.

Benjamin Randall and Margaret Mordantt Randall had nine children, of whom Benjamin, the subject of this story, was the oldest.

Respecting social, military, and political rank, at his birth, February 7, 1749, Benjamin, later called Elder Randall, entered into an honorable heritage. His parents were people of intelligence, education, and refinement. His Grandfather Walton was of good English stock. As a military man, this

Benjamin Randall

Walton was ensign in 1691, major at the attack of Fort Royal in 1707, and colonel of the Rangers raised the next winter for guarding the New Hampshire coast in the Indian troubles of the times. As a civilian, he was judge of the Court of Common Pleas in 1635-1638; judge of the Supreme Court in 1638-1639, and again in 1716-1737. He received the commission of Councillor to the Governor in 1716, which position he probably held during the remainder of his life, for he stood as senior councillor in 1733.

Others of note descended from the same stock, some of whom contend that the line passing through the Walton vein can be traced back through several distinguished nobles to a monarch. Mr. Randall would often talk facetiously to his children of their noble blood as a motive for their consistent behavior.

In early youth Benjamin enjoyed such means for mental culture as were afforded by the public schools, from which, with his own efforts and parental aid, he obtained a

Benjamin Randall

"good commercial education." This was supplemented by general reading, close study, personal experience, and observation, so that he became, in an all-round sense, well educated for his age and times.

As soon as he began to form definite notions of the divine character and requirements, his mind took a decidedly religious turn. He says:

At the age of five I seldom closed my eyes in sleep at night without prayer to God in such language as would best express the feelings of my heart. In those exercises I would often be affected to tears. From that time I practised secret prayer and was always led to pray on my knees or prostrate on my face, though I had never seen any one pray in these attitudes, or heard that any particular attitude had been enjoined as a duty.

In the church of his parents, both in family and public devotions, prayer was offered in the standing attitude. From his earliest remembrance, Benjamin also *en-*

[7]

Benjamin Randall

joyed sanctuary services. With him, church attendance was never regarded as an irksome duty, but always as a glad privilege.

Benjamin's father was a sea-captain, and a portion of his youth was spent as a cabin-boy on board his father's ship. By this experience the circle of his vision was enlarged, and his acquaintance with different localities and different people was extended. His desire for self-improvement led him to turn all such opportunities to good account.

But a seafaring life included conditions that were not congenial to his refined and sensitive nature. He did not enjoy the society to which he was restricted on shipboard. Indeed, he was constantly shocked by the coarse jokes and profanity of the sailors. As his father safeguarded him as much as possible, and as he kept up his daily Bible readings and devotions, the youth was uncontaminated. Yet he longed for conditions that would enable him to choose his social, intellectual, and religious environment.

[8]

Benjamin Randall

When Benjamin was nearly eighteen years of age, in response to his request, his father apprenticed him to a sailmaker in Portsmouth, with whom he remained till he was twenty-one. In connection with this apprenticeship, after strict fidelity to business, which he rendered, he found opportunities for study which he improved.

But, by an accidental occurrence, as it might seem to a casual observer, young Randall took up a branch of secular business for which his practical knowledge of sailmaking had measurably prepared him, and which did not depend for its success upon location in a seaboard town. And this is the way it happened:

Awhile previous to his majority, Benjamin's father purchased for him a " dress-up " suit from rich, light-colored material, worn by society gentlemen at that time. Attired in this, he attended a social gathering where the chairs had been recently " done over " in dark paint, not yet hard dry. On reaching home Randall found his garments irregularly mottled. He did not want his father to know of the accident. But how could he conceal it?

In this dilemma he called his own resourcefulness to the rescue. Having at hand all needed furnishings, and having learned their use at sea and at sailmaking, he retired to his room, where " positively no admittance " was to be allowed, and set about the task of changing the leopard's spots. Fortunately, the goods were reversible. He ripped the garments apart and turned them with such complete success in workmanship that no visible traces of his accident remained. Thus commenced his efforts as a tailor, at which trade he became proficient, and to which he turned in after years, as Paul turned to his tent-making, when necessity was upon him, for honorable support.

All who impartially read the religious history of the eighteenth century, and later, must admit that our country owes much to the parents of Benjamin Randall for giving it such a son, and for training him so strictly

Benjamin Randall

in the Puritanic system—a system well adapted to bringing the whole person under the restraints of proper discipline, begetting in him the habit of cheerfully submitting to the inevitable and courageously doing obvious duty.

From home care and home culture the youth was enabled to carry into the world those habits of neatness and order, of industry and uprightness which ever proved invaluable treasures, opening to him doors of acceptable entrance and success, which might have remained closed to others less favored. Thus they laid in him a solid foundation upon which the grace of God built a noble superstructure.

II

F ROM early childhood, through youth to manhood, Benjamin Randall had sustained the habit of daily Scripture reading and prayer. His external life had been in strict conformity to the standards of morals held and taught by his ancestral church—"The Standing Order." But soon after passing his majority he entered a religious experience, to him entirely new.

In 1769-1770, George Whitefield made the last of his several evangelistic tours in this country. He arrived at Portsmouth, New Hampshire, on the twenty-third of September, 1770. But, personally, Mr. Randall was in neither mental nor spiritual condition to give him a cordial welcome. Not that he lacked interest in anything that might, in his opinion, make for public righteousness, but, as judged by the " Standing Order," the cause of religion had suffered somewhat in that vicinity by certain traveling preachers. Mr. Randall's sympathy with the established church, and his natural love of order, roused his antagonism against all preachers except the settled Congregational clergy.

The next day after the arrival of Whitefield, Randall, prompted largely by curiosity, followed the crowd into what was called the " Great Meeting-house," but with the resolution that the preaching of the evangelist should have no effect on him. Thus fortified, he heard Whitefield several times, the last being on Friday before the death of the great evangelist, which occurred on the following Sunday.

A record found in Randall's journal has this: " The next Sabbath, September thirtieth, our minister went to Portsmouth to preach in the Great Meeting-house, taking me with him." Then no bridge connected New Castle with the mainland, hence, the

Benjamin Randall

minister needed some one to row him over to Portsmouth that day for his meeting. Randall, being an expert on the water, and very companionable withal, was selected for that purpose. In view of what occurred later, this arrangement seemed providential.

At noon that day, while Randall was conversing with a friend, a mounted herald approached, proclaiming as he rode: " Mr. Whitefield is dead! Died this morning at Newburyport, about six o'clock!" This announcement greatly shocked Mr. Randall. The sermons he had heard from the lips of Mr. Whitefield were passed in review. His mind was quickened, his conscience was aroused. He conceded the truth of those sermons and felt self-condemned that he had allowed prejudice to delay his appreciation so long.

Respecting the announcement of the herald, Randall says:

As I heard this voice, an arrow from the Almighty pierced my heart. Mr. Whitefield was a man of God and I have spoken re-

Benjamin Randall

proachfully of him. That voice is now silent in death. I would sacrifice anything if I could hear it again. But that cannot be. With what a loss have I met! On reaching home, I took my room to mourn in solitude over my condition. My former religion seemed altogether worthless.

On October fifteenth, while musing on my condition, I fell into the following train of thought: "Once I was company for almost every one, but now for none. I took pleasure in the world, but now there remains nothing of that. All things appear insipid. I, who used to enjoy so much in prayer, now cannot offer one petition." Yet, on second thought, I know I did pray, though I did not enjoy prayer as formerly. While thus musing, Hebrews 9: 26 came to my mind: " But now once in the end of the world hath he appeared to put away sin by the sacrifice of himself." I was in such deep meditation that the words passed without particular notice. They came up the second time, however; then I began to think, What can the passage mean? *"But now once in the end of the world hath he appeared to put away sin by the sacrifice of himself."*

Benjamin Randall

While meditating upon the text my burden rolled off, leaving me calm and peaceful. As my faith grasped the meaning of the text I gave glory to God. And what a joy filled my soul! I could now see in Jesus Christ a blessed sacrifice for sin, to the full satisfaction of divine justice. How the character of Jesus shone in my soul! For a time I could do nothing but repeat the name of Jesus. Jesus! Jesus!! It seemed to me that if I had a thousand souls I could trust them all in his hands. I saw in him universal love, a universal atonement, a universal call to man, and felt confident that none could ever perish but those who refused to obey.

Then what love I felt for all mankind— longing that they too might share in the fulness which I saw so extensive and so free. What pity flowed into my soul for poor sinners, whom I saw to be in the gall of bitterness and the bonds of iniquity.

Now the question may arise as to Randall's piety previous to this awakening under the preaching of Whitefield. Let us see. The habit of daily Bible reading, daily

Benjamin Randall

prayer, regular attendance upon church services, and the faithful observance of all means of grace known to him, had been sustained from early childhood, through the years of youth, up to manhood.

In the exuberance of youth he had indulged in a few social pastimes, but none not approved by his parents and family church. Up to Whitefield's visit to Portsmouth, Randall's deportment had been above reproach. Respecting his internal condition, he might have said with Paul: "I have lived in all good conscience before God unto this day." In the anguish of his soul, when struggling for clearer evidence of divine acceptance, he refers to the fact that formerly he "enjoyed so much in prayer." Now, only those who are in right relations to God, *enjoy* prayer. His mental antagonism to Mr. Whitefield was not occasioned by the doctrines that were preached, but by his prejudice against all traveling preachers.

The experiences of Mr. Randall, though not common, are not unknown to history.

c　　　　[17]

Benjamin Randall

They place him in a class with some other religious leaders. Among representative cases, reference might be made to the decisive hours in the lives of Augustine, Luther, and John Wesley. Of these, the experiences of John Wesley were, in many respects, duplicated by those of Randall.

John Wesley was well born. The piety he learned and imbibed at his mother's knee he carried through educational processes into sacred orders. But, it is more than probable that, with all his early excellences—and he had many—he placed undue emphasis upon good works as a condition of saving grace. One of his biographers, referring to this period, says: " He was narrowly introspective and exclusively bent on saving his own soul."

Wesley's mission to Georgia, though not a total failure, was far from a brilliant success. The Georgian colonists did not take kindly to his methods, and the Indians he had hoped to convert wanted none of his religion. After a brief effort he returned to

Benjamin Randall

England, thoroughly disgusted—with himself. On his voyage home he wrote in his "Journal": "I, who went to America to convert others, was never converted myself. I am a child of wrath, an heir of hell." Wesley afterward retracted these extreme statements; but they show his mood on returning from his Georgian mission.

But if a prophet had whispered in the ear of John Wesley, he might have said: "Be of good cheer! It is the divine order that suffering should be the price of usefulness. The Lord would show thee how great things thou must suffer for his name's sake. Only be thou strong and very courageous. Thou shalt yet renew the religious life of thy beloved England. Thy disciples shall yet spread over the same America that witnessed thy humiliation. Thou shalt yet have the world for thy parish."

For a while after Wesley reached England he preached a faith for which he confessed himself to be waiting. But after a few months he got the blessing he sought,

Benjamin Randall

and a paragraph quoted from his journal gives the manner of it:

In the evening I went unwillingly to a society (of Moravians) in Aldersgate Street, London, where one was reading Luther's preface to the Epistle to the Romans. About a quarter before nine, while he was describing the change which God works in the heart, through faith in Christ, I felt my heart strangely warmed. I felt I did trust Christ, Christ alone, for my salvation; and an assurance was given me that he had taken away my sins—even mine—and saved me from the law of sin and death.

Where there is evidence of former piety up to crises such as here described, the most recent psychology regards these sudden transitions from a lower to a higher, a perturbed to a restful, spiritual state, however caused, as incidents to mark the ingress of new truths and new motives otherwise inaccessible. This philosophy seems to have application to both Wesley and Randall.

But our special interest centers in Ran-

Benjamin Randall

dall. May we not account for this crisis in
his religious experience in a way entirely
consistent with a concession to his former
piety and God's gracious purposes concern-
ing him? It seems evident that Randall had
been pious from his childhood up to this
crisis. But it seems quite as evident that
his piety had been self-centered, and therefore of a low order. His dominant motive
seems to have been to save his own soul and
make sure of heaven. If he had died during
those years he would doubtless have been
saved, as were probably some of the " Pillar Saints " and other ascetics, who never
knew till they got to heaven how they failed,
because of their narrowness, of a more
abundant entrance.

Benjamin Randall was a chosen vessel
unto the Lord, to bear his name before the
Gentiles and God's Israel. But before he
could receive his commission he must be
lifted from a lower to a higher plane of
Christian life. He must know, as he had
never known before, the exceeding sinful-

[21]

ness of sin. He must realize as he had never realized before, its hatefulness in the sight of God. He must have a fuller realization, than he had ever had before, of the sweet peace that follows deliverance from sin, and the ecstatic joy of a heart filled with God's abounding grace.

Some of the processes of this uplift were so agonizing that it is not strange that Randall was at times led to question the genuineness of his former piety. But short of these experiences, Randall could not have stood with God upon the mount. Short of these experiences he could not have had a vision of his future field of labor. Short of these experiences he could not have efficiently filled the interim between the mount of vision and the glory beyond.

III

M R. RANDALL spent the summer of
1771 at his trade, in Marblehead and
Salem.   He lived a watchful and devoted
life, and attended religious services strictly
with his own sect.   During this time he had
an offer which gave flattering prospects of
soon making him a man of wealth.   This,
however, he declined to accept, and for reasons that, at the time, he could neither un-
derstand nor explain.   In referring to the
matter he says: " But since, I have seen that
God overruled in the matter, having other
and more important work for me in prospect."

Randall returned to New Castle in October, hired a sail-loft, and set up business for
himself. On the twenty-eighth day of November he was united in marriage with Miss

Benjamin Randall

Joanna Oram, youngest daughter of Capt. Robert Oram, of Kittery, Maine. Captain Oram was a native of Topsham, England. In early manhood he migrated to America and landed in the South, but after a brief stay he settled at Kittery, married Joanna Mitchell and, as was the manner of the times, raised up a family of which Joanna, born March 2, 1748, became the wife of Benjamin Randall.

The record Randall made in his " Journal " respecting the good providences of God in the person of his wife, he never had occasion to revise: " I believe she was the gift of God to me, and that no woman was ever better suited to the place in which she was to stand. May God have the praise."

When the newly married pair commenced housekeeping they erected the family altar, which stood till death broke in upon the union.

In the fall of 1772 Mr. Randall called on his pastor and informed him of the desire, on the part of himself and wife, to become

Benjamin Randall

members of the church, and received the reply: " Well, Mr. Randall, I am glad you have come to a sense of your duty; I will propound you next Sabbath." On saying this, the pastor was about to leave the room. But the applicant, having anticipated that he might be examined on his Christian experience and views of religious doctrine, asked for such advice as might seem needful, preparatory to such an important step. To this no answer came. Mr. Randall persisted, however, as he tells us:

After a pause in the conversation I broke the silence and, in short, related to him what the Lord had done for my soul. To this he made no reply, but looked as though he thought it strange. I requested that I might see the covenant and have it explained, that I might be sure that I understood its import. He permitted me to take a copy home for examination. In response to my invitation, he promised to call and interview my wife on the matter. This call he made the next day, staying perhaps an hour, but saying nothing on religious sub-

Benjamin Randall

jects during the time. When rising to leave, he turned to Mrs. Randall and said: " Your husband tells me you have a mind to join the church. I will propound you to-morrow."

Mr. and Mrs. Randall were duly received to membership in the Congregational church at New Castle. But Mr. Randall soon found that he had united with a people whose religious experience was not like his own—a people who neither shared with him his heavenly emotions nor his burning zeal for the salvation of souls. But let him speak for himself:

On better acquaintance, I found that the church had neither order nor discipline. Men of intemperate and corrupt habits were allowed to come each month to the communion without reproof. This discovery, with a view of the condition in which those were who made no pretense to piety, caused me such great distress of mind that at times it seemed as though I could not live. My food became tasteless, and sleep departed from my eyes. By night, when whole families were sleeping, I would walk the streets, stop before their doors, lamenting their condition, and praying God in their behalf.

As opportunity offered, Randall talked with his brethren respecting the importance of a deeper work of grace in the church and efforts for the salvation of those outside. Thus matters continued till the spring of 1774, when Randall felt impelled to go forward in a more open and decided effort.

He conceived the plan of opening meetings in which the people could listen to the reading of printed sermons and exercise their gifts in prayer, exhortation, and singing. This suggestion, when confided to Randall's special sympathizers, received their hearty approval.

The first move was to get the consent of their pastor, which was given with apparent cordiality, and with a promise of occasional attendance himself. These new gatherings caused no little excitement in the place. Whatever the motive on the part of the people, they were largely attended and there were indications of a general revival.

The local pastor attended but once, and then showed signs of disapproval. From later manifestations it became evident that he was jealous of Mr. Randall for starting another religious center which, though intended as a helping hand of the church, was regarded by the pastor as a rival. This feeling of alienation on the part of the pastor ripened into coldness, and finally antagonism.

As Mr. Randall loved his ancestral church and desired its welfare, as he loved his native town and desired its evangelization, as he loved his pastor and desired to be a worker together with him for public betterment, the developments described in the foregoing paragraphs were the cause of bitter grief to his soul. But they opened his eyes clearly to the fact that it would be neither for his own benefit nor for the glory of God for him to continue his membership with that church. So, after making the

matter a subject of fasting and prayer, he
sadly, but decisively, withdrew.

How sad, alarmingly sad, was the religious condition of that community! What
a demand for a radical reform! But the
conditions of reformation were already
present and operative. A small cloud was
already in the heavens, and the sound of
abundance of rain would soon be heard.

IV

IN common with many patriots of his times, Mr. Randall had a military experience. The clouds of the Revolution, so long and so sullenly gathering, had at length shut down over the country with terrific gloom. Indeed, on the plains of Lexington, the war had already begun. There was not one drop of Tory blood coursing through the veins of young Randall, and with all the ardor of his nature he responded to his country's call for patriots.

According to an article in the Adjutant-general's Department of New Hampshire, awhile previous to the real outbreak, from apprehensions of danger on our coast, certain of the militia were called to muster at New Castle. Among these, Mr. Randall was enrolled in the company of Capt. John

Benjamin Randall

Parsons. But the fear soon subsided, and the company was dismissed.

Early in the summer of 1775 a British man-of-war hove in sight and lay near New Castle. As the town was wholly unprotected, the people very naturally feared that it might wantonly be laid in ashes as had been Falmouth, now Portland, and other coast towns that year.

Mr. Randall and his brethren held a special meeting for fasting and prayer that the impending danger might be averted. What influence this observance exerted we may never know. But New Castle was saved and the warship sailed away.

In October the danger from the enemy became so threatening that the people fled from New Castle into the country. Randall was opposed to going; but, as his wife was in such fear, he assented and moved his family to the upper part of Kittery. As a sufficient number of troops had arrived to guard the place, in November he removed his family to New Castle, and immediately

Benjamin Randall

enlisted for two months as assistant commissary. As a matter of curiosity, and as an illustration of his characteristic attention to details, a scrap of his commissary account, found among his papers, is here reproduced:

An Inventory of Sundries Received in Store for the Use of Troops

40 iron pots, 3 iron kettles, 6 frying-pans, 27 water-pails, 29 wooden bowls and platters, 1 earthen bowl, 2 wooden ladles, 1 shovel, 1 hoe, 1 skillet with handle broken, 2 iron bars, 5 powder-barrels, 2 pairs iron hinges and gudgeons, 1 stone hammer, 1 hand-saw, 1 powder canister, 2 qt. tin measures, 1 pint do., 1 gill do., 1 ax, 1 small piece of rope.

Taken Out of Stock Since

5 iron pots, 4 frying-pans, 4 water-pails, 1 ax. The same for the soldiers at Fort Hancock. 1 pot at Mrs. Pritchard's, 1 do. at Mrs. Tarlton's, 1 do. at Fort Hancock, 1 pot at the old fort.

Benjamin Randall

By reference to State documents it is ascertained that, after his commissary service, Mr. Randall reenlisted, September 10, 1776, as sergeant in the company of Captain Calf, regiment of Col. Pierce Lang. By putting accounts together, it is found that in different capacities Mr. Randall served in the Revolutionary struggle nearly a year and a half. It is known that during the first two months of service he received two pounds, about ten dollars, per month. It is probable that later his pay was made to correspond with his official advancement.

Respecting his religious state while in the army, Mr. Randall says:

All the time I was a soldier I enjoyed much of the divine presence. Indeed, I never lived nearer to God than during that campaign experience.

Josiah Magoon, a fellow soldier with Randall, but later a Free Baptist minister, left this record:

Benjamin Randall

Mr. Randall was a highly intelligent, active, and upright young man. His habits were excellent; he, with his brethren, kept up a meeting in the place, which caused the remark in camp that " Randall means to be a preacher." His influence among the soldiers was of a most salutary character. He was accustomed to visit the sick and administer to them the consolations of religion; indeed, doing largely the duties of a chaplain. Thus many a desponding heart was cheered and made strong by his efforts.

But some of the scoffing class for a time took occasion to deride him for what he was doing. To this, however, Colonel Mooney brought an effectual end. This officer was a stern man and, withal, a great lover of order and uprightness. He admired the untiring efforts, gratuitously bestowed by Mr. Randall, for bettering the condition of those called out for the defense of their country. Hearing of these indignities, at the next parade he called the attention of the regiment to the matter, expressing his deep chagrin at the fact that any of his soldiers

Benjamin Randall

should show themselves so vile and debased. He stated with unmistakable words and accents that a repetition of that abuse would be visited with severe punishment. This had the effect desired.

These facts about Colonel Mooney were stated by his son John, then a youth in army service, in attendance on his father, but years later Judge Mooney of New Hampton.

V

THOUGH separated from the church which did not accept kindly his efforts of service, Mr. Randall did not long remain isolated. His yearnings of soul for congenial associations were soon gratified. Those of like desires for higher attainments in Christian life soon gathered about him. The very few of this class belonging to the church he had left soon followed his example and also withdrew. Those doing this clung to each other with great tenacity. Though few in numbers, and the objects of much persecution, they trusted in God and pressed forward. They also opened meetings for religious services by themselves. Among evidences of God's approval they were favored with a gradual increase, both in numbers and Christian graces.

Benjamin Randall

Notwithstanding the excitements incidental to martial surroundings, Mr. Randall began to feel strong convictions that he ought to preach the gospel. These convictions followed him wherever he went or however engaged.

The time that remained to Mr. Randall, aside from the exactions of his official duties, he devoted to the study of the Bible, with special reference to the subject of baptism. He became convinced that believers are the only proper subjects of the ordinance, and that immersion is the only scriptural mode of administration. In short, he found that to be consistent with God's word he must come out a Baptist. Though he wanted to know the truth as to this and all other matters pertaining to doctrine, it was with sadness that he made this discovery. He says:

Though it was like taking away a right hand to give up my former views on this point, I durst not hold them where I found not a " Thus saith the Lord."

Benjamin Randall

Mr. Randall's convictions respecting the ministry, to which reference has been made, grew more and more absorbing. A quotation from his journal is illustrative:

One day while I was attending to my usual duties, and at the same time bewailing the state of the ungodly, the power of God seemed to impress me to go out and warn them. But, while pleading against this because of my insufficiency, these words came impressively to my mind, " Set them before them." On turning to my Bible, the first words that caught my eye were these: " And when he had taken the five loaves and two fishes, he looked up to heaven, and blessed and brake the loaves, and gave them to his disciples to set before them." Considering how the disciples remonstrated because they had so little, and how Christ multiplied it, my pleas were all silenced.

Soon after becoming settled on the doctrine of baptism, Mr. Randall's own duty in the matter confronted him. He at first thought of going to Stratham and seeking baptism at the hand of Doctor Shepard.

Benjamin Randall

Then, again, he felt that he must consult, at least, his brother Trefethren on the subject. Hence he set off one evening for that purpose. On the way he met the object of his visit coming to interview him on the same subject. Both were greatly surprised and overjoyed at the coincidence. They interpreted this as providential, and by it their faith was much strengthened. They concluded, however, to keep this change of views to themselves until its declaration might be made without endangering division in their company, and planned to go to some other place and receive baptism. But before an opportunity for this presented, it seemed to Mr. Randall wise to modify their plans so far as to test the sentiments of others associated with them. But here is his own story about it:

We were met in one of our private fasts, and were enjoying a blessed meeting. I thought I would attempt to ascertain the minds of all present respecting baptism, and commenced thus: "What a poor little com-

pany of speckled birds we are! We belong
to no society or denomination of people. I
wonder if, on inquiry, we could tell what to
call ourselves. Well, if anything, I am a
Baptist." "So am I," exclaimed Brother
Trefethren. "So am I," "And so am I,"
"And so am I," came from every one present. What a surprise filled our minds!
When conversing freely on the matter, we
found that all at the same time had been at
the same school, under the same Teacher,
and had come to the same conclusions; not
one having mentioned the matter to his fellow—for we had no man to teach us.

Prof. A. T. Robertson has said: " Given
an open Bible, an open mind, and a conscience in good working order, and we will
have a Baptist." Among many others, the
experiences of John Bunyan, Adoniram Judson, Benjamin Randall, and his company of
the Lord's disciples are corroborative.

In a further account of that meeting of
discovery, Randall says:

How did our hearts rejoice together! We
shouted and praised God for his wonderful

ways, and for the increase of our union and fellowship. The desire was unanimously expressed that an administrator be sent for to baptize us all at home. But before that could be brought about, report came that Mr. William Hooper was to be ordained at Berwick, and Mr. Trefethren and I decided to attend.

On leaving home we had no thought of being baptized on that occasion. But, as Mr. Hooper was to administer the ordinance to others that day, after his ordination, the impression came upon us with great power to embrace the opportunity and not wait for a more convenient season. So we were then, October 14, 1776, and there baptized, and, like the eunuch of Ethiopia, returned home rejoicing.

At his baptism Mr. Randall united with the Baptist church at Berwick. Mr. Hooper soon after evinced his pastoral faithfulness by writing him a letter. The response to this, and also a letter to the church written a day later, are interesting as specimens of the general style of letter-writing in Colonial

times, and as exponents of the excellent
spirit that characterized Mr. Randall, and
show how profoundly satisfied he was with
his newly found religious home, the Baptist
church.

VI

FROM READING SERMONS TO PREACHING
1777

THE brethren had continued their meetings in the form adopted at the beginning, Randall taking the lead in reading and
other exercises. But one evening as they
were closing, one of the attendants called
out: "Mr. Randall, I am tired of hearing
you read old sermons. If you will not
preach to us, do leave that off and read the
Bible instead." The expression, "If you
will not preach to us," deeply impressed Mr.
Randall's mind, leading him to infer that
others also knew of his duty.

On reflection Mr. Randall concluded to
comply with the request as far as it concerned Bible reading, but not as a step toward preaching. In pursuance of this purpose, at their next meeting he opened his
Bible at John 13 : 1, and read: "Now be-

fore the feast of the Passover, when Jesus knew that his hour was come," etc. After reading the first verse, instead of going to the next, he paused to give a few words by way of exposition. The text opened to his mind such a rich train of thought that he continued at some length, when he became suddenly conscious that he was doing what he did not intend to do. That is, he found himself expounding the Scriptures or, as some might say, preaching. With this awakening he sat down, covered with confusion.

The next day his chagrin was greatly increased by the current report that " Randall preached last night." He resolved not to venture in this direction again, but to return to his former course. Hence, for their next meeting he took a volume of Watts' sermons with him. On opening the service he was doubtful which to read, the Bible or a sermon. In his hesitation, he took up first one, then the other. Thus he shifted a few times, but finally settled upon the sermons, one of which he began to read. But we will let him describe results:

As I read I began to die—as to springs of life in my soul; and the more I read, the more I felt the life departing. At length I thought, should I venture a line further the Lord would depart and give me up to hardness of heart and blindness of mind. What feelings were mine! I threw down the book and broke in confession. With tears I told the people how the Lord had made it manifest to me, for the last two years, that it was my duty to preach the gospel. I told them that I had been like Jonah, who attempted to flee away from the presence of the Lord. But now I was, by the grace of God, resolved to be obedient, and give myself up to his service as long as I lived

The next day Mr. Randall wrote a covenant in which he laid himself and his all upon the altar for service or sacrifice, as it might please God. After this consecration he received a renewal of his commission and a fresh baptism of the Holy Spirit. His former timidity about preaching now entirely left him. Instead of centering his thoughts upon his own incapacity, he was enabled more fully to realize God's exhaustless resources, and to grasp more firmly his promises of support. This experience occurred some time in March, 1777.

At their next meeting Mr. Randall took the Bible with all needful confidence and gave his first sermon, choosing for his text Revelation 3 : 12: " Him that overcometh will I make a pillar in the temple of my God, and he shall go no more out." This effort was greatly to the edification of his hearers, and gave high promise as to the future.

The stand thus taken by Mr. Randall caused much excitement in the place. A certain class gave bold threats of personal violence if he should persist in his undertaking. Yet he was graciously preserved and went fearlessly on, holding meetings both day and night, preaching on an average four times a week.

For several weeks he saw no special results of his efforts except an increasing

Benjamin Randall

congregation and the spiritual quickening of
his associate workers. What he sought and
prayed for was the salvation of sinners, and
it is not strange that he was getting somewhat discouraged because he saw no special
move on their part. But God was working
out his gracious purposes, and would soon
give abundant proof that the prayers of his
servant were heard and that his labors were
not in vain.

On a Sabbath in the spring of 1777, Mr.
Randall preached from Titus 2: 14: "Who
gave himself for us, that he might redeem
us from all iniquity." This greatly moved
his audience, especially the unconverted portion of it. As the assembly was passing out
at the close, he heard a voice in the street,
toward which the people were centering. On
pressing through the crowd he found a
woman in great distress on account of her
sins. As he approached, she exclaimed: "O
Mr. Randall, what shall I do? I am a miser-
able, undone sinner!"

In reply Mr. Randall said, "Come into

Benjamin Randall

the house and I will tell you." The people speedily reassembled, and he instructed the inquirer as to the proper course for her to pursue. That is, to submit herself wholly to God, and earnestly pray for the forgiveness of her sins. This she did then and there, and her example was followed by others. This event, so extraordinary at the time, produced a powerful effect upon the congregation. Some mourned for their sins, and some praised God for the manifestations of his grace.

VII

FOR a while the work bore down all opposition. People flocked to hear the new preacher, and the revival spread till some thirty were hopefully converted. Then opposition commenced in open demonstration. The enemies of equal rights and the exercise of religious liberty began to feel alarmed, and judged that something must be done to arrest the revival. In Mr. Randall's report of it we have this:

Now persecution grew very hot, and such threatening language was used that I really felt my life in danger. But I gave myself to prayer, and the Lord wonderfully protected me. As I was walking the street one day, a brickbat was thrown at me with such violence that it was broken in pieces on hitting the opposite fence. The aim was

E   [49]

Benjamin Randall

so accurate that it brushed the hair on my head. Had I been two inches farther back, results must have been fatal. May eternal praise be given to Him who shielded my life! I was about turning my head to see whence the missile came and who threw it, but thought I will not, I don't want to know. Now I can pray, "Lay not this sin to his charge." Should I know, perhaps when I see him I might feel some hardness.

One evening a number came and stood before my door, reviling and cursing me, with the threat that they would throw me into the river. These, I think, were from a neighboring town.

Once I appointed a meeting in New Castle-on-the-Main, where a goodly number assembled. One of the selectmen from Rye and one from New Castle, with tar and feathers, and each leading a mob, met at a gate where they supposed I should pass, purposing to tar and feather me. But I happened to go to the place by water. They were so exasperated at their disappointment that they applied the material intended for me to the posts and beams of the gate, where it remained a long time as a memorial of

Benjamin Randall

their wicked purpose. Many a passer-by
had them in derision.

One occasion more of attempted mob violence must suffice here. The same summer,
by invitation, Mr. Randall appointed to
preach in a town not far away. But previous to the appointed day he received several intimations of threats from certain of
the people that, should he attempt to fill his
appointment, they would mob him. The
evening previous to the designated time, a
brother came expressly to charge him not
to venture upon an attempt to hold the service, as the town was in an uproar. But he
would go, let the consequences be what they
might. He was not to be daunted. His
commission made no provision for danger
that might lie between him and duty.

Calling at a friend's on the way, near the
border of the town, he met a report that, the
day previous, parties had been about with a
drum, beating for volunteers; that a band
of forty men was collected at a tavern he

was to pass; that a man had offered this mob
a barrel of rum if they would kill Mr. Randall. To this he responded in his characteristic aptness:

That is the devil's old regiment. He
raised forty men before to kill brother Paul.
But he missed it then, and I believe he will
now. I feel that God has called me to
preach in that town, and I am resolved to
go. It would be better for me to die many
times over, could that be, than to desert the
cause of Christ and bring reproach upon it.

He adds:

All who came in said what they could to
dissuade me from venturing forward, and I
received no encouragement but from my
blessed Master.

Finally the woman of the house where he
was to preach came by a crossway, with
face bathed in tears, and besought him not
to proceed, as the mob might kill him and do
her and her house much harm. To this he
replied:

Benjamin Randall

Don't be afraid, woman; you shall not be injured because of me. I must go into your town to preach the gospel, but can do without a house to preach in. I am willing to stand under a tree and there address any who will hear me.

Accompanied by a few friends, Mr. Randall went by the tavern where the mob was waiting, sure enough, but no violence was offered him. When he reached the place of his appointment he found the man of the house calm and unintimidated by threats; so it was mutually agreed to hold the service where appointed—in the house.

After waiting awhile for the mob, Mr. Randall commenced his sermon, taking for his text Acts 13 : 46: " Then Paul and Barnabas waxed bold, and said, It was necessary that the word of God should first have been spoken to you: but seeing ye put it :from you, and judge yourselves unworthy of everlasting life, lo, we turn to the Gentiles." Soon after the opening of the services the dreaded mob drew up in line in

Benjamin Randall

front of the house. At this the women took fright and ran out of the house, causing some commotion. But the men remained quiet, and the speaker proceeded without the least intimidation. The same spirit that inspired God's servants, mentioned in the text, sustained and emboldened Mr. Randall. He says:

As soon as I saw them I felt a most blessed degree of God's power drop into my soul. I felt assured that it would be impossible for them to touch my person; or, if tearing the house down over my head, for one stick of its timbers to fall on me. I felt completely shielded by the omnipotent hand.

Soon after the arrival of the company a tempestuous shower arose, producing a scene, perhaps in a faint degree, resembling that witnessed on Mount Sinai at the giving of the law. While the speaker was proclaiming the truth as powerfully as he could within, the lightning's flash and the thunder's roar spoke in appalling accents without.

Benjamin Randall

Just as the meeting closed the shower ceased, and the thunder was heard only in the distance. Mr. Randall went out and shook hands with several of the men, not one of the company giving him an ungentlemanly word. The company soon retreated, and Mr. Randall's friends, supposing all danger past, left him to go unattended to an evening appointment on his way home.

He had not proceeded far before entering a pine thicket, where he caught sight of the band. The time, between sunset and dark, the lonely thicket, the mob blinded by bigotry and frenzied by rum, combined to give an uncanny suggestion of danger; but he halted not. If the God of Joshua whispered in his ear, the message might have been in substance the same as that given to his ancient servant: "As I was with Moses, so will I be with thee. I will not fail thee nor forsake thee. Turn not to the right hand or to the left. Have not I commanded thee? Be strong and of good courage; be not afraid, neither be thou dismayed; for the

Benjamin Randall

Lord thy God is with thee whithersoever thou goest." In any case, Mr. Randall rode fearlessly forward. On his approach, the mob opened to the right and left, allowing him ample room and, with uncovered heads, said " Good night! " as he passed.

This occurrence at once illustrates Mr. Randall's indomitable courage and the declaration of the psalmist: " Surely the wrath of man shall praise thee: the remainder of wrath shalt thou restrain." He attributed this deliverance to the providence and grace of God. This is evinced by the exclamation that closes this account of it:

Oh, the infinite goodness of God to me! What shall I render unto him for all his goodness? I will offer the sacrifice of thanksgiving, and call upon the name of the Lord.

VIII

DURING the summer of 1777 Mr. Randall commenced traveling farther into country places on preaching tours. He labored considerably in Madbury and adjacent places, and saw a goodly number converted. On one of these excursions certain men from New Durham heard him, and extended an invitation for him to visit that place and preach to their people. In compliance, he shortly after bent his course thither. As he went, he preached at intervening towns, and saw rich displays of God's converting grace in several of them. But his own description of that journey justifies its reproduction:

It was a wonderful journey. Wherever I went the blessed Master was with me. The power of God fell on old and young. Sinners were crying for mercy, and many were led to rejoice in God all through Barrington. But some opposed me in great rage, called after me, reviled, threatened, but the Lord preserved me.

It appears that the part of the town where Randall's labors were most particularly blessed was then called Crown Point, but since Strafford Corner. Reverend Hooper, of Berwick, soon followed Randall, baptizing the converts and gathering them into a branch of his church.

Mr. Randall's preaching at New Durham caused quite an awakening among the people. One result was that they united in extending a call to him to move into the town and become their minister. To this solicitation, however, at the time, he gave no encouragement. During the fall, after his return from an eastern journey, Mr. Randall again visited New Durham. Finding the people still urgent in their request before made, he answered them that, could he know it to be God's will, he would comply.

Benjamin Randall

After a meeting of fasting and prayer for divine guidance, all came to the conclusion that "the thing proceeded from the Lord." Hence, the citizens, by a committee, waited on him, with proposals for settlement. This was a proposal that Mr. Randall become the settled minister of the town, to spend his life there, and that his salary be paid from the town treasury, as was the custom in the case of the regular clergy of the times.

To this committee Mr. Randall gave an affirmative answer as to his locating in town, but made it clear that he could not consider further conditions of settlement; that it was not his purpose to confine his ministrations wholly to one locality, but to hold himself at liberty to serve others withal, as God might direct. In accordance with a few simple details, mutually agreed upon, the matter was settled.

Mr. Randall, with his family, left New Castle March 23, 1778, and arrived at his destined home on the twenty-sixth of the same month. Thus he settled for life, making New Durham the base of his subsequent ministrations.

New Durham is located about twenty-five miles from Concord, in a northeasterly direction. It was granted to proprietors in 1759 and incorporated in 1764. It was first settled in about 1762, largely by people from Durham, New Hampshire, hence it took the name New Durham. It is said that the original grant included what is now the town of Alton.

Mr. Randall was the second minister to locate in the town, Nathaniel Porter, D. D., a Congregationalist, having been his predecessor. Doctor Porter served awhile as chaplain in the Revolutionary army, but on returning demanded that the people pay him the same as though he had not been absent. They regarded the demand as unjust; and for this, or other reasons, he resigned.

While Mr. Porter was in New Durham the people built a meeting-house. This became a part of Mr. Randall's New Durham

Benjamin Randall

inheritance. Since Randall's time it has been remodeled into a town house, and as such it still stands. Mr. Randall located his home on what is called " The Ridge."

This elevation covers a panoramic view, combining great beauty and grandeur. The western outlook is somewhat limited by beautiful wooded hills. Away in the north, some hundred miles distant, appears Mount Washington, with his head towering among the clouds, and looking down with undisputed majesty upon his humbler fellows, which, as sentinels, stand about him.

The intervening space is beautifully diversified with hills and dales, hamlets and villages, running waters and lakes. To the southeast the prospect stretches as far as the eye can reach, giving a view of the lower towns. And at favorable times the view covers a long reach of the coast and ships far out at sea.

In his arrangements with the citizens of New Durham, Mr. Randall gave his first recorded protest against the legal mode of

Benjamin Randall

settling ministers then in vogue. He would have no man taxed or compelled to contribute for his support. He would have everything pertaining to worship and religious support left to the volition of the people.

For the accomplishment of this end he had determined to do what he could. Though only one, his voice should be heard and his example set in that direction. We are by no means to infer by this that he ignored the teachings of the Scriptures respecting the support of the gospel ministry. But rather, like Paul who, from present necessity, and perhaps more from the corrective power of example, wrought, in a few cases, at his handicraft, so Mr. Randall decided upon his present course simply as a temporary matter, to be changed as Providence might indicate.

Mr. Randall had a good trade, and later a small farm. To one or both of these he resorted as necessity required, but so managed as to secure time for study and extensive evangelistic work.

IX

CALLED TO ANSWER AS TO DOCTRINE
1778-1779

DURING 1778, in connection with his local labors, Mr. Randall preached to some extent in other places. Revivals attended his efforts, especially in Gilmanton, Loudon, and Canterbury. In connection with these many were converted, of whom some entered the ministry.

But, though settled in a place combining such physical attractions, congenial associations, and the witness of God's approval, Mr. Randall was not exempt from harassing conditions. He was doomed to feel, as never before, the cutting force of the language by which the psalmist gave expression to some of his experiences: " It was not an enemy that reproached me; then I could have borne it: neither was it he that hated me that did magnify himself against

[63]

me; then I would have hid myself from him. But it was thou, a man mine equal. We took sweet counsel together, and walked unto the house of God in company."

Up to this time, within the sphere of Mr. Randall's acquaintance, the Baptists had moved forward in one united band, cherishing a common interest in the promotion of their general cause. They had all shared alike in the odium that the intolerant spirit of the age was accustomed to heap upon those dissenting from the dominant sect, and were all feeling the rigor of unjust religious laws. This outside pressure had tended to drive them together, and cement their hearts more firmly in the bonds of Christian affection.

But that good-fellowship was not to continue. For while some, like Randall, adhered to the doctrine of free grace for all who would accept salvation, others held the doctrine that God, by his sovereign will, had determined that, while a certain number must be saved, others, both adults and in-

fants, must be lost, and all—as they would
contend—for the glory of God! Some
would preach that there were infants in hell,
not a span long!

The extremes of Calvinism, as above described, had now, to some extent, crept into
the Baptist denomination, especially in New
England. It does not appear, however, that
this doctrine had, as yet, been made a matter
of controversy; at least, not in Randall's
circle. We do not learn that up to this time
he had said anything about these distinctive
views, but we infer that he had passed them
quietly by. It is probable that Randall's
mind was crowded with the ideas of salvation full, free, and possible to all, and the
importance of offering that salvation to the
largest number, in the least possible time.

The first attack on Mr. Randall was by an
aged minister, who called on him publicly to
state why he did not preach the distinctive
views of Calvin. His laconic answer was,
" Because I do not believe them." " Then,"
Mr. Randall says, " he fell into a discussion

with me upon the matter. But it only served to set us farther apart." The date of this interview was probably March, 1779.

This attack necessarily brought the subject before Mr. Randall's mind as never before, drawing him into a closer study of the points in dispute, and to a more careful survey of the whole system. This resulted in a clearer and deeper conviction that what he had preached was the truth.

But still he found certain texts, notably in Romans, that he could not explain quite to his own satisfaction. Yet, seeing that the whole tenor of those passages was in his favor, he, like a rational man, concluded that when correctly understood these Scriptures must be found in harmony with the doctrine of free salvation, and that their Calvinistic construction arose from a false system of philosophy. He says:

The more they disputed with me on these points, the stronger I grew in my sentiments; for it drove me to searching the Scriptures with greater diligence, and to

Benjamin Randall

pray more earnestly to God for a correct understanding of their meaning.

In July, 1779, Mr. Randall was summoned before a meeting, held for the purpose, at a Baptist church in Lower Gilmanton, to answer for his alleged doctrinal errors. He there met his inquisitors during a two days' debate. But so clearly and forcibly did he sustain his views that all combined could not confute his arguments. At the close, his most prominent and zealous accuser thus proclaimed: " I have no fellowship for Brother Randall in his principles." To this Mr. Randall replied:

It makes no difference to me by whom I am disowned, so long as the Lord owns me. And now let him be God who answers by fire, and that people be his people whom he owns and blesses.

A little later Mr. Randall was again arraigned, with Daniel Lord, at a public meeting in Madbury, to answer for what some

Benjamin Randall

called his wrong sentiments, to which he briefly alludes in his journal thus:

They had us in a great meeting-house, before a large congregation, and disputed with us as long as they saw fit. Then they let us go without owning us or disowning us. I applied to the church to which I belonged for dismission, but they would not grant it. Neither, to my knowledge, did they ever appoint a committee to labor with me, or put me under censure—so they let us alone.

Here note: Mr. Randall was not expelled from the Baptist denomination.

Thus harassed, Mr. Randall found himself in an undesirable situation. But he could not violate his convictions of truth and consent to preach Calvinism. Hence, he saw no alternative but to follow Paul's example in regard to Barnabas—step aside from these ultra-Calvinists, and pursue the path which he believed to be divinely marked out for his own footsteps.

But, in making this move, it is evident

that he had no purpose or anticipation of founding a separate sect. He still claimed a place in the Baptist ranks, and full loyalty to Baptist principles. He was fully opposed to any division then, and until several years later, when it seemed a necessity.

It was one of the greatest trials of Mr. Randall's life that anything should have occurred to strain the sympathetic relations between himself and his former brethren. Surely no just reason could be produced why he, and those of like views, should at that time leave the Baptist fold. They were not the aggressors, and could claim a clear right of possession by inheritance.

Mr. Randall and those of like faith were cherishing views over which no controversy had arisen for many centuries after the dawn of the Christian era; views too, which were held and taught by the General Baptists of England, the early Baptist churches of our Southern States, Rhode Island, Connecticut, and more or less in the Middle States. The West was not then developed.

Benjamin Randall

It is believed by those whose opinions command respect, that hyper-Calvinism was especially assertive at this time in New Hampshire and Maine, and that the doctrines held and preached by Mr. Randall would not have been antagonized if proclaimed in any other section of our country.

James A. Howe, D. D., late Dean of Bates College Divinity School, was a Free Baptist representative at the World's Parliament of Religions, held in connection with the Columbian Exposition, at Chicago, in 1893, and presented to that parliament a summarized history of the Free Baptists. A paragraph of this has fitting place in this connection. Doctor Howe says:

The first Baptist church recognized in English history was of the General or Free Baptist order, and antedated the first Particular Baptist church by a score of years. For a long period the General Baptists continued the larger and more influential part of English Baptists, and therefore we should expect that, among the earliest Baptist

Benjamin Randall

churches in America, no small number would be of this persuasion; as, in fact, they were; the church planted by Roger Williams being properly reckoned as the first. With numerous churches centrally placed, they gave early promise of a large development in our country, a promise that only needed fulfilment to have taken away any occasion for the rise of the Free Baptists as a separate people. But this golden opportunity was not improved.

X

IF WISDOM AND COMITY HAD DOMINATED
"PERHAPS THEY WOULDN'T"

THE Rev. Doctor Brierly, in writing of
the providential closing and opening
of doors, though referring to the experience
of others, describes the crisis that Mr. Randall had reached. He says:

How often do we seem, in our private
fortunes, to be brought to a loose end! Some
source of supply has been stopped; some
door of career has suddenly been slammed in
our face. The well-defined track we had followed has all at once disappeared. We are
faced with the wilderness, wherein we must
strike a road of our own. Most of us who
have lived any time in the world have had
a touch of that experience. It is one of the
greatest tests of character. We have been
good enough for routine; what good are we
for this crisis of the unexpected?

It is here that strong men prove their
strength. How often has that moment

Benjamin Randall

proved the starting-point of mightiest
things! It was so with Wesley when he
found himself in hopeless conflict with the
Anglican authorities, and he must choose
some other way. And with General Booth,
his true successor, when on that fateful
morning he left the New Connection Conference, his terms rejected, his career as one
of its ministers closed, and himself in the
face of a new, untried world. Spurgeon
had his moment when, by the strangest of
accidents, he missed a collegiate training.
But these men " made good."

When Whitelaw Reid was American ambassador to Great Britain he was very popular with the highest social and political cir-
cles. On one occasion, when he was dining
as a guest in common with the high-titled,
including King Edward, one present had the
bad taste to say, addressing his remarks to
the ambassador: " The American colonies
belonged to England, and had no right to
establish a separate government." For a
moment the breathless attention of all present centered on Mr. Reid. But his diplo-

macy was equal to the occasion. He courteously responded: "If King George had been as wise as his royal great-grandson," bowing low to Edward, "perhaps they wouldn't."

Now, if any are of opinion that those of Free Baptist sentiments ought not to have established a separate organization, it might be answered: If those represented by the ministers who tried Mr. Randall for heresy had been as wise and courteous as the leading men of the present Baptist body, "perhaps they wouldn't."

However that may be, they *did,* and no just biography of Benjamin Randall can be written without giving at least a passing statement, not only of the fact, but of the reasons why. But it will be a help to mutual charity if it be remembered that those were times which, in all matters pertaining to religious difference, polemics had the ascendency over comity.

Now we make haste to rejoice with representatives of high Baptist authority that

Benjamin Randall

" the reasons why " are dying, if not already *dead* issues. From an editorial which appeared in a June, 1905, issue of " The Watchman," a Baptist paper, the following paragraph is selected:

At the time of the separation from the Baptists by Benjamin Randall in 1780, the controversy was wholly about Calvinism. Mr. Randall was accused of preaching anti-Calvinistic doctrines; and the number of his followers increased until, in 1827, the Freewill Baptist General Conference was founded. It is only necessary to mention this controversy to show how obsolete it is to-day. The Freewill Baptists dropped the middle word from their title years ago, and are now known as simply Free Baptists. And there are probably as many among Baptists who would refuse to be called Calvinists as there are among the Free Baptists. This, the original cause of separation, has simply taken itself out of the way, and calls for no consideration whatever.

At a meeting of the Joint Committee of Baptists and Free Baptists, held at Brook-

[75]

Benjamin Randall

lyn, November 22, 1905, Nathan E. Wood, D. D., president of Newton Theological Seminary, was chosen chairman. In the course of his introductory remarks, President Wood said:

In spirit the Baptist churches were never more tolerant than to-day. At the time when Free Baptists went away from us hyper-Calvinism prevailed, and Free Baptists had grounds for going away, and ought to have gone. But we have no hyper-Calvinism now, but a very moderate Calvinism. On the matter of communion there has been no great change in the last twenty years. On immersion we stand as rigid as ever we did. The Baptists made a tremendous fight on baptism, and close communion was an expression of it.

The editorial referred to in a preceding paragraph has this respecting communion:

It is doubtful if there is a Baptist church in the North to-day which would refuse to allow a Christian, who wishes to do so, to partake of the Lord's Supper with it.

[76]

Benjamin Randall

In the last chapter of Vedder's very excellent "History of the Baptists" we find these statements:

Though Baptists have thus powerfully influenced other bodies of Christians, it would be a mistake to infer that they have themselves escaped modifications in belief and practice through the influence of other Christian brethren. That both Calvinism and Arminianism have been so modified as to bear little relation to the systems once passing under their names, is so well understood, and so little likely to be questioned, that it is not worth while to waste space in more than a statement of the fact. Each has reacted on the other, and between the latest statements of the two opposing systems a critical student can discern little more than a difference of emphasis.

XI

A S one of the results of the doctrinal
discussions, to which reference has
been made, early in 1779, a church, embodied by Elder Edward Lock, composed of
people in Loudon and Canterbury, New
Hampshire, declared themselves Arminian.
The church had largely or wholly arisen
from Mr. Randall's labors in that vicinity
the previous year.

In August of the same year the brethren
at Crown Point, who had stood as a branch
of the Berwick church, under Elder Hooper,
embodied themselves into a church and also
declared themselves Arminian. Elder To-
zier Lord, having been previously ordained
at Lebanon, Maine, by Dr. Samuel Shepard
and others, espoused the free-grace cause,
withdrew from the Calvinistic church, and

in the same fall became a member of the
Crown Point church as its pastor.

In March, 1780, Mr. Randall presented
himself and was received to membership
in the Crown Point church. During this
spring season a precious work of grace was
in progress at New Durham. The time
having arrived when the interests of the
cause demanded the ordination of Mr. Randall, it was regarded as a special providence
that the way for this step had been prepared by the establishment of those two
Free churches.

It appears that the idea of the brethren
was, that to render an ordination valid beyond all question, at least two regularly ordained ministers, in good standing in some
church, should lay hands on the candidate;
while lay brethren might properly assist.
True, they could point to precedents where,
in very urgent, exceptional cases, even
among those who were sticklers for good
form, one duly ordained might, with lay
assistants, do the work of ordination. But

Benjamin Randall

here were two churches properly constituted, with their pastors duly qualified. Hence, they were prepared to comply with best accepted usages for induction to the gospel ministry.

In arranging for the ordination of Mr. Randall, the Crown Point church consistently took the lead. The time agreed upon was Wednesday, April 5, 1780; place, New Durham. The Crown Point church chose its pastor and one lay delegate to attend, and invited the Loudon and Canterbury church to do the same, which it did.

The council met on the day appointed and proceeded to their work, setting apart the candidate in due form to the work of an evangelist. Elder Lord preached the sermon from Acts 13 : 2, 3: "As they ministered to the Lord, and fasted, the Holy Ghost said, Separate me Barnabas and Saul for the work whereunto I have called them. And when they had fasted and prayed, and laid their hands on them, they sent them away." Lord also gave the charge. Lock

Benjamin Randall

gave the hand of fellowship and probably offered the prayer of consecration. Thus, so far as ecclesiastical forms were concerned, Mr. Randall was duly qualified for the work of the gospel ministry.

The title " elder " is variously used in the Bible. The same is also true respecting its use in some modern religious bodies. In the Baptist denomination, in the eighteenth century, more commonly than now, it was given to gospel ministers. This title, which was given to Mr. Randall by virtue of his ordination, and which he carried and honored for thirty years, may in the following pages be prefixed to his name.

XII

NEW DURHAM CHURCH FOUNDED
1780

SOON after his ordination, Elder Randall called a meeting of his New Durham brethren, preparatory to organizing
them into church relationship. After duly
deliberating upon the matter, it was agreed
that they thus organize and appoint Mr.
Randall a committee to draft the requisite
articles of faith and covenant, and present
the same at a future meeting.

In accordance with due notice, that meeting occurred June 30, 1780. After devotional services, the first business was the report of Elder Randall on Articles of Faith
and Church Covenant. These articles were
then read, intelligently considered, and de-
liberately adopted. This done, the candidates, four men and three women, came forward, signed the covenant, and as an ex-

[82]

Benjamin Randall

pression of their fellowship and union, joined hands. Then Elder Randall presented the sacred Scriptures to them as their only rule of faith and practice, extended to them the hand of fellowship, and while all knelt offered a prayer that the Spirit of God might consecrate them to his service.

Though not accepting any prefix to the Baptist name till twenty years later, thus was organized in due form the first Free Baptist church.

The articles of faith then adopted are lost beyond recovery. They were written on the first leaf of the records, which leaf has been torn off. But when, by whom, or for what purpose, it will probably never be known. While regretting the loss of these articles, we have the satisfaction of knowing substantially the doctrines they contained. Elder Randall stamped those doctrines indelibly upon the minds of his people. The fathers stated and restated them until, with little expansion, they were published in their present form. As the same is true of the

[83]

church covenant, though that is preserved, neither need be recorded here.

The new church did not choose officers till early in September, when others had united. Then a full Board was chosen, with Elder Randall as pastor. Respecting the pastor, it was understood that he should be at liberty to go on evangelistic tours as he might interpret the will of God.

They entered into an agreement that they would maintain weekly meetings of a devotional nature. These should be sustained by voluntary prayer, singing, and exhortation by the brethren and sisters present. All were expected to attend when practicable, and each take some part in the services. Should the pastor at any time be absent from public worship, and no other minister be present to supply his place, the social-meeting plan was to be operative. Thereby regular worship was to be maintained each Sabbath, whether a preacher was present or not.

In this arrangement was evinced much

true Christian philosophy. Mr. Randall would not only have a God-called and a God-furnished ministry, but he would also bring up the laity of the church to a high plane of Christian living and Christian activity.

They also entered into agreement to hold a meeting on a special day of each month; hence the name Monthly Meeting. Unless prevented by what would keep him from ordinary business, each member was held in duty bound to attend, and there give an outline of his religious experience during the previous month, or interim since last attendance. At the close of any Monthly Meeting appropriate church business might have consideration.

The establishment of the New Durham church laid the foundation of the Free Baptist denomination. But why not regard the Canterbury and Loudon church, or the one at Crown Point, the foundation church? True, one had withdrawn from the Calvinistic body and adopted free sentiments, and the other had been founded on similar principles. But both stood as independent organizations, without connecting bonds with any other. And neither was a nucleus around which accretions should be made. Both of these churches soon lost their visibility, while the New Durham church became a nucleus around which other churches soon gathered. Hence, we must ever regard the gathering at New Durham as the mother church.

XIII

THE SCRIPTURES OPENED
1780

THOUGH highly prospered in his work, Mr. Randall experienced no little distress of mind for a time, because of the alienation of his former brethren. His attachment was so strong that his separation from them left a deep wound in his heart. He greatly felt the need of fraternal associations and fraternal counsel.

Then, again, he would suffer great perplexity respecting those texts which he could not construe to his own satisfaction. He knew they must harmonize with the general tenor of the Scriptures, but this was not fully satisfactory. The question would often arise, " What do these texts mean? " Then, again, the feeling, " I must know." But how could he obtain the knowledge? He knew of no living person to whom he

Benjamin Randall

might resort for aid or comfort. As to books, in the meager supply at that time, the Bible almost alone taught a full and free salvation.

In this extremity, Mr. Randall could go to none but his Bible and his God, with any hope of finding a solution to the questions that burdened him. To these sources of information he turned with all possible concentration of thought and devoutness of feeling. Here we have an illustration of the proverb that " Man's extremity is God's opportunity." But we will let Mr. Randall tell of the very extraordinary experience through which he passed:

Some time in July (1780), being in great trial of mind because of such texts, and desiring solitude, I walked to a remote place on my farm, where I had a field of corn, which I entered. My soul being in great agony, I sat down upon a rock, and prayed that my heavenly Father would teach me. All at once it seemed as if the Lord denied my request. This increased my trial, and I said, "Lord, why may I not be

Benjamin Randall

taught?" I then saw that my heart needed much purifying and refining. I said, "Lord, here am I, take me, and do with me as thou wilt."

And oh, the flaming power that instantly possessed my soul! It would be impossible to give one an adequate idea of the experience, unless he had passed through the same. The power increased in my soul, until it stripped me of everything as to my affections. I tried to recollect my brethren and connections, but had no feeling save of the awful majesty of God, before whom I sank, as it were, into nothing.

Then it appeared that I saw a white robe brought and put over me, which completely covered me, and I appeared as white as snow. A perfect calm, an awful reverence pervaded my soul. A Bible was then presented before the eyes of my mind, and I heard a still, small voice saying, "Look therein." I looked in at the beginning of Genesis, and out at the close of Revelation.

To state the remainder of this vision in fewer words than his account, Mr. Randall saw the seals of those difficult texts all

Benjamin Randall

unloosed, and their explanations were seen to be in perfect harmony with a general atonement and a universal call. He adds:

My soul has never been in any trial about the meaning of those Scriptures since. After passing through this experience the vision was withdrawn. I came to myself sitting on the rock in profuse perspiration, and so weak I could hardly sit up. I observed the sun, and estimated that I had been in this exercise about an hour and a half; and whether in the body or out of the body, I never could tell.

This experience of Mr. Randall was certainly remarkable. The extent to which the Holy Spirit may have been operative in producing it will be measured by the religious experience of those who judge. As a help to correct judgment, it should be borne in mind that the whole trend of scriptural teaching is to the effect that God, in the economy of his grace, has made provision for his helpful manifestations to those in extremities such as Mr. Randall had

Benjamin Randall

reached; and that " more things are wrought
by prayer than this world dreams of."

The subjoined statements of Samuel D.
Robbins, D. D., aline with this doctrine:

There is a communion with God in
which the soul feels the presence of the un-
seen One, in the profound depths of his being, with vivid distinctness and a holy
reverence, such as no words can describe.
There is a state of union with God—I do
not say often reached, yet it has been attained in this world—in which all the past
and present and future seem reconciled, and
eternity is won and enjoyed; and God and
man, earth and heaven, with all their mys-
teries, are apprehended in truth as they lie
in the mind of the Infinite.

Mr. Randall was sure that in that vision
he was especially favored with divine assistance. However it may be accounted for, he
somehow at that time obtained views on
those Scriptures that had perplexed him,
essentially differing from constructions then
current, but which now have general acceptance with the religious world.

XIV

SOON after Elder Randall's divine illu-
mination, in response to an invitation,
he went on a mission tour to Maine. In his
account of it he says:

I visited Little Falls on the Saco River,
and there experienced a precious work of
grace, which spread about for a number of
miles in that region, and many came to the
services.

On November fifth the Little Falls friends
wrote to the New Durham church for one
to be sent to their aid. About the same
time a delegate, in the person of one of their
deacons, came from a band of professing
Christians in Gorham, Maine, requesting the
privilege of fellowship as a sister church
with the New Durham brethren.

[92]

Benjamin Randall

These requests were interpreted as imperative calls that must not be disregarded. The church responded by delegating to their aid its pastor and Robert Boody, as traveling companion, who at once set off on their mission. As to the result of their Gorham visit, records are silent. But the visit to Little Falls resulted in strengthening the religious interest there, and the formation of a church of a hundred members.

In February, 1781, Mr. Randall, having received an invitation from one Jewell, a Baptist brother, visited Tamworth, New Hampshire, then but recently settled. One of the results of this visit was a revival in which a goodly number were converted and a church organized. This church was gathered in the westerly part of the town, about the region later called Stevenson's Hill.

The same season Mr. Randall gathered another church in Barrington, probably in the section over the " Blue Hills," and extending somewhat into Barnstead. A part of this locality has since been called North

Benjamin Randall

Strafford. It is probable that his own labors had been largely instrumental in preparing the material for this church. As to who else may have preached there about that time we have no record. These tokens of divine approval greatly encouraged Mr. Randall, and stimulated him to increased zeal in his labors. His journal holds the following record:

Early in the fall of 1781 I was deeply impressed with a desire to take a religious tour eastward as far as the Kennebec River. But discouraging conditions confronted me, it being near the close of the war and money scarce, of which I had but little. Then too, I would be a stranger in a strange land, and it was unusual for a minister to go about and preach, such being regarded with suspicion on the part of many.

At length, however, Mr. Randall's objections were overcome, and he went, as thus described:

On the last day of September I set off alone and traveled to Saco River, where I

Benjamin Randall

found a brother willing to accompany me to the end of my journey. The Lord granted us his presence and prospered us on our way. The people showed us much kindness as we traveled.

Mr. Randall crossed the Kennebec at Georgetown, and in the evening of October first held a meeting in that region on Ker's Island. The people gave respectful attention and expressed a desire to hear him again. Randall complied with the request the next forenoon. At this meeting many were brought under conviction, were at length converted, and became substantial, devoted Christians.

That afternoon Mr. Randall preached his first sermon in Woolwich. This proved to be an eventful occasion. Here lived a number of devoted Christians of free sentiments. They were intelligent, and withal of good standing in public esteem. But they had become tired of the old, lifeless religious forms among them, and had been earnestly praying for some evangelist to visit them and

[95]

Benjamin Randall

preach a free salvation and a heartfelt religion. This stranger's visit seemed in answer to their prayers. His sermon, and the unction with which he spoke, appeared as of God.

These people were much like sheep, long left uncared for, but now permitted to hear the shepherd's voice. They could hardly contain their joy. If at the time the Holy Spirit did not fall upon them, as under the preaching of Peter, they were made to drink from the cup of happiness in Christ as deeply as human beings may reasonably expect to until released from earthly bondage.

The rumors of this meeting spread extensively the next day, and a crowd gathered for the next service. Mr. Randall then preached from Philippians 2 : 9: " Wherefore God hath highly exalted him, and given him a name which is above every name." The word seemed like fire and hammer to many flinty hearts. The work of grace here begun spread through the region with great power.

Benjamin Randall

At the close of these meetings Mr. Randall baptized five persons. This was a novel scene for that place. Though about three hundred were present, not more than three or four had ever seen a baptism administered by immersion.

Returning to Parker's Island, Randall found the work spreading prosperously. After laboring here a few days, he left and spent the Sabbath in Woolwich, where he baptized a number and organized a church. Before leaving this region it is probable that Mr. Randall formed a church at Georgetown, Squam Island, and at Durham; for he speaks of having a church at each of these places soon after his return.

Mr. Randall was absent on this eastern tour thirty-seven days, held forty-seven meetings, and traveled about four hundred miles. He soon left again in answer to a call from Gorham and Scarboro. God blessed his labors, especially at the latter place, where many were converted, baptized, and added to the Little Falls church.

Benjamin Randall

About this time Samuel Weeks, a Baptist minister of East Parsonsfield, Maine, with his church, came out and took a stand with Randall. So also a body called the Gray and Gloucester church.

These accessions, thus rapidly made, were at once a comfort and a care to Mr. Randall. These churches were all organized on the same model as at New Durham, and looked to the same undershepherd for general oversight. Still, each stood in an independent state, having no connecting bonds, except what existed in the fact that each had embraced the same general views, and taken the same platform in its structure. But conditions were now rapidly tending to the organized union that soon followed.

XV

THE year 1782 held for Elder Randall experiences both sad and joyous. On account of the long and painful sickness of his father-in-law, who died at his residence on the fourth of July, he spent the first several months at home and in the vicinity. During this time some of the churches suffered somewhat for lack of his general supervision.

In the spring two emissaries of Ann Lee, the prophetess of Shakerism, had come from Watervliet, New York, then the headquarters of the cult in this country, and from their teachings the delusion had spread over portions of New Hampshire and Maine. All churches in the track of this delusion suffered from its blighting influence; but, for lack of pastors at that time, this was es-

Benjamin Randall

pecially true of Free Baptists. Mr. Randall stoutly opposed this cult, exposed its errors, and tried to counteract its destructive work.

But, while Free Baptist interests were thus attended with deep trials in some places, prosperity was experienced in others. This season a church in Gorham took its stand with Randall. This was a body of respectable brethren, and became a strong, influential people, and for many years sustained a controlling influence in that region.

In September Mr. Randall again visited his Kennebec plantation, to find the work spreading blessedly through that entire part of the country. Besides meetings for worship, he held sessions for business where needed.

In October Daniel Hibbard, formerly a Baptist minister, but recently allied with Randall, wrote to New Durham from Little Falls for help. In answer, Randall went to render aid on the fourteenth of November. But no record is found as to the conditions or the producing cause thereof.

Benjamin Randall

In religious matters, Randall closed the year 1782 much as Washington did in his struggle for national liberty. He had suffered reverses and achieved victories; thus showing that in Church as in State a campaign will have its vicissitudes.

Early in January the brethren in Canterbury and Loudon, not swept away by Shakerism, sent a feeling request to the New Durham church for aid. In response, the pastor and others were delegated to visit them. The efforts of these messengers tended to revive somewhat the drooping spirits of this almost disheartened people, and initial measures were taken looking to reorganization.

On March second Mr. Randall was prostrated by a fever which continued for more than two months. For a time he could not raise his head from his pillow, and it was feared by many that he would not recover. During this time he enjoyed the abiding presence and comfort of the Holy Spirit. His recovery was slow, being retarded, no doubt, by his great anxiety for the religious condition of the community. But strength at length returned, and with it Mr. Randall devoted himself anew to gospel work.

In the early part of July, on request of the scattered Crown Point brethren, Randall went to their aid. He there found eleven desirous of coming together to work in gospel order. He reorganized them into a church, and as a pledge of good faith they signed a covenant which Randall formulated for their future government.

On the twenty-sixth of September Mr. Randall started for another eastern tour. He visited the churches at Little Falls, Woolwich, Dunston, Georgetown, and Edgecomb, finding them in a flourishing condition. They had received large additions and were steadfast in the faith. Proceeding still farther east, he preached at New Castle, on the Damariscotta River. Then, crossing the river, he held meetings in Bristol and on Rutherford's Isle. All these efforts were attended with glorious results.

Benjamin Randall

Homeward bound, Randall stopped for a night at Major Larabee's, on New Meadow's River in Brunswick, and there held an evening meeting which was well attended. In response to the solicitations of the people, he held several meetings at different places in that vicinity, at which professed Christians were revived and many souls were converted.

On arriving at Little Falls, Randall met several brethren in conference respecting best methods for future work. He had become satisfied that the churches, for their fullest development and greatest usefulness, needed to enter into a combination for mutual help. But what the combination should be, and how it could be brought about, was not so clear. He could find no precedents suited to his needs.

The nation was just securing its release from monarchical rule to government by the people. The public mind was filled with democratic principles. These principles were taking form for the government of the new

Benjamin Randall

nation. Being loyal to his country, Randall could but be averse to anything in religious government contrary to the independence of the churches. The importance of candid deliberation and wise planning was felt by all present.

This conference was made up of Randall, Pelatiah Tingley, Daniel Hibbard, and several laymen. As the names of these two ministers, now associated with Randall, will appear occasionally in connection with the denominational development, it is fitting that they have more than a passing mention.

Daniel Hibbard was one of the first Baptist ministers to be ordained in Maine. But on acquaintance with Free Baptist principles he allied himself with Mr. Randall.

Pelatiah Tingley was graduated from Yale College in 1761, studied theology two years, and then commenced to preach with the Congregationalists. Having preached over a year at Gorham, Maine, as a candidate, he gave a negative answer to the invitation of the town to settle there in 1776. Later, he conducted religious services at New Market, New Hampshire. It was summer, very warm, and the sanctuary was ventilated for comfort. While he was reading his sermon, a gust of wind carried a part of his manuscript sailing through an open window. This proved to be an important event of his life. He retired from that meeting with the resolution never again to attempt preaching till he had attained to a gospel that winds could not take from him. He sought God with prayer and tears till he received a baptism of the Holy Spirit. On careful study, Mr. Tingley became convinced that sprinkling is not baptism, and that none but true believers are fit subjects. Thus he came out a Baptist. He embraced the doctrinal sentiments of Randall, and was a factor much needed at the time, especially in the work of organization.

But to return to the work of the conference. At this session it is probable that Mr. Randall presented a plan of organization

Benjamin Randall

and suggested a name for the body. The plan provided for the combination in one body of all the Free Baptist churches; that this body should meet four times a year, and therefore be called a Quarterly Meeting. It should consist of delegates and others from the constituent churches. It should discuss and devise ways and means leading to united church effort and the highest degree of efficiency.

It was agreed that these plans be laid before the respective churches for their consideration. Their conclusions were to be reported at a meeting to be held on Saturday, the seventh day of December, when, if reports were favorable, the movement would be fully inaugurated.

Mr. Randall was absent on this eastern tour fifty-seven days, traveled about five hundred miles, and attended sixty-one meetings.

At the time appointed the delegates met at Little Falls. Enthusiastic approvals of the plan were received from the churches.

Benjamin Randall

The meeting organized by the choice of Randall for moderator and Tingley for clerk. After deliberate consideration it was decided to adopt the plan and proceed to the organization of the body it contemplated. It was agreed that the body should be known as the Baptist Quarterly Meeting.

At this permanent organization Randall was chosen Quarterly Meeting clerk, which position he held for life. The regular sessions were to be held on the first Saturday of specified months, as follows: March, in New Gloucester; June, in New Durham; September, in Woolwich; and December, in Little Falls. This was to be the order till otherwise arranged.

At this session some needed advice was given to the Little Falls church, and Joseph Judkins was licensed to preach.

By request, an adjourned session was held at Dunston, December tenth, and with other business, the brethren there were organized into a church. The session also issued a circular letter to all the constituent churches,

Benjamin Randall

signed by Randall and Tingley. This letter urged upon the churches local union, co-operation with the Quarterly Meeting, and watchfulness against religious delusions. Here they evidently had in mind Shakerism.

Quarterly Meeting arrangements with the Free Baptists have since that time undergone some important modifications. But, though this was a day of small things, its work is not to be despised. It was the beginning of an organized system which culminated in the General Conference. And it has been conceded by those whose opinions command respect, that, all things considered, Free Baptists have one of the finest systems of ecclesiastical government extant.

Some conception of Mr. Randall's early labors may be gathered from the fact that, during the first three and a half years of his ministry, in addition to local work and broadcast seed-sowing, he had organized thirteen churches of the Free Baptist faith, and drawn to his side four ordained ministers—Lord, Weeks, Hibbard, and Tingley.

Benjamin Randall

These were all men of intelligence, consecration, and power. They were all well furnished for the work to which the Master was calling them.

Furthermore, those churches contained a goodly number among the laity who were intelligent and fairly well educated for the times, whose powers were in process of development. Through consistent living, the study of the Scriptures, and the constant exercise of their "gifts," they were becoming well qualified for the duties of the ministry, to which they were at length admitted. Many others of the private membership were, in the same way, advancing to greater efficiency as Christian workers.

XVI

THE new year, 1784, found Mr. Randall confined to his bed because of sickness. But his energy and interest in the churches prompted him to resume work while yet quite feeble. With Isaac Townsend as companion, he attended the March session of the Quarterly Meeting, which was held at New Gloucester. The attendance was large, and the constituent churches reported hearty approval of the Quarterly Meeting plan and organization.

As this was the first regular session since the organization of the body, and as its order of procedure was for many years regarded as a model, it seems fitting that it have a somewhat detailed report. It appears that Mr. Randall had, with characteristic forecast, worked out a program for the

[110]

session which, subject to such changes as the nature of the case might suggest, was adopted by the conference. And here we have it:

QUARTERLY MEETING PROGRAM

Saturday Afternoon

1. Devotional. Consisting of prayer, singing, and if time favors, exhortation.
2. Choice of officers. Moderator, clerk, and committees.
3. Letters and verbal reports from constituent churches.
4. Examination of members as to doctrine, fellowship, and so forth.
5. Efforts to restore harmony, where such efforts may be needed.

Saturday Evening

Preaching, followed by exhortation and general worship.

Sunday Services

Morning. Prayer and general devotions.
Forenoon. Preaching.

Benjamin Randall

Afternoon. Preaching.

Evening. Preaching.

Devotional services immediately preceding or immediately following sermons, as conditions may suggest.

Monday

Devotional. Unfinished business. New business named in letters or otherwise presented.

All business interspersed with much prayer, singing, and devotions.

It appears here that while Mr. Randall, for economy of time and the discipline of good order, would have these assemblies governed by prearrangement of a general nature, he would not foist upon them inflexible rules. The wisdom of this system was proved by its harmonious working, with slight changes to suit conditions, for a whole century.

Another measure for the benefit of the churches, inaugurated at this session, and continued for many years, was the issuance

of a Quarterly Meeting circular epistle.
This method of reaching the entire member-
ship had its origin in the fertile brain of
Mr. Randall.

The quarterly letter generally contained
a summarized statement of session proceedings, any special business requiring the attention of the local church, and doctrinal
statements or corrections, with many injunc-
tions to hearty piety and right living. Print-
ing-presses were not then so generally distributed over the country as now, and tran-
scripts were made by pen. Randall was a
ready writer, and was not only author, for
the most part, of these letters, but probably
made most of the reproductions, although
as churches increased and burdens multiplied, a part of the clerical work fell to Tingley and others. As soon as possible after
the Quarterly Meeting session a copy of the
epistle was sent to each of the constituent
churches, to be read in the presence of the
next assembly. The unifying influence of
these epistles, in fellowship, doctrine, and

church methods, was great, but cannot be measured by exact calculation.

The September Quarterly Meeting was held at Woolwich. Randall served as moderator and Tingley as clerk. After routine business had been disposed of, Shakerism, which was still proving rather troublesome, both in New Hampshire and in Maine, was considered. It was agreed that in all the constituent churches, October thirteenth should be observed as a day of fasting and prayer, " that God would sweep away this delusion by the breath of his Spirit."

This session proved a rich blessing to the cause of religion in the east. There, brethren of similar religious sentiments met, who had been strangers to each other and unaware of what was being accomplished for Christ in the general field. There they were enabled to take larger views of Christianity than ever before, and could unitedly devise broader plans for work in which mutual helpfulness might result.

Benjamin Randall

A special feature of this session was the alertness of the churches in conforming to the arrangement of reporting by letter. The pile of these letters before us would make an interesting chapter of church history, as illustrative of the times in which they were written. But the determined limits of this work will admit of only a summarized statement. They were interesting as exponents of Christian union, biblical sentiment, gospel order, and intelligent formulation. Furthermore, they gave a hint as to the general intelligence and culture of the people who then embraced the doctrines that Mr. Randall held and taught.

During the year 1784 Mr. Randall traveled in his religious work over a thousand miles, attended more than three hundred meetings of worship, besides those of business, and preached on an average a sermon each day.

As may be seen later, 1785 was a busy year for Mr. Randall. In addition to his accustomed visits to the churches and at-

Benjamin Randall

tendance at Quarterly Meetings, he pushed his work into regions beyond.

A few cases of discipline required attention, but for the most part the churches were orderly, vigorous, and cheered by increased membership. Quarterly Meeting sessions were well attended, their proceedings harmonious, and their influence beneficial to communities entertaining them. In some cases, revivals beginning in these meetings spread to adjacent towns.

In one session the question was asked as to the relations of the ruling elder to the church and ministry. The answer given at the next session was that the ruling elder is a church officer between a deacon and a teaching elder, or pastor; that he might conduct general religious meetings, and, by consent of the local church, administer the ordinances in the absence of a teaching elder or pastor. During the early years of our denomination, the ruling elder filled an important niche in church economy. But as the instalment of settled pastors became more common, his office, with its necessity, ceased.

During this year Joseph Boody was ordained a ruling elder, and John Whitney a teaching elder. Also the New Canaan, later Lincolnville, church was received.

A question submitted to the September session was, " Is it proper to commune with one who, though not having been immersed, gives evidence of a change of heart, and daily leads a Christian life? " Answer by unanimous vote, less one, " It is."

Among the good things in one of the general epistles this year, ministers are exhorted to watchfulness, humility, and purity of life. In another, the unconverted are warned against a hope of salvation simply on the ground that its possibility had been provided through Christ. In referring to this so-called liberal doctrine the statement runs thus:

This is a tenet we fear has destroyed its thousands, though it is a groundless doctrine, and can easily be confuted by the

Benjamin Randall

Scriptures. The plain assertion is before us, that, " Except ye be converted . . . ye shall not enter the kingdom of heaven."

Mr. Randall closes his record for 1785 with this sentence:

I have traveled this year about twelve hundred miles in religious work, and attended over five hundred meetings.

At the opening of 1786 the Randall family was saddened by the sickness and death of Mrs. Oram, Mrs. Randall's mother, who died in that home February tenth.

A little later Mr. Randall visited the churches in western Maine. He found some of these churches suffering from certain discordant elements, some enjoying revival grace, and others rejoicing over recent accessions. By all he was heartily welcomed, and to all he preached the Lord's gospel with freedom.

Some business of special interest was considered and transacted at the June session, held at New Durham. Measures were taken

Benjamin Randall

to create what, for the lack of a better name, might be called an emergency fund. The proposed fund was not intended for ministerial support, but to meet other ordinary and needful expenses, among which would be the aiding of any brother or sister who, by sickness or otherwise, might fall in need. Such a fund was raised; it may have further mention later.

The Calvinistic churches of New Hampshire and Maine had formed a union somewhat similar to that into which Mr. Randall's churches had entered, only its associated meetings, instead of being quarterly, were held but once a year, and the body was called the New Hampshire Baptist Association.

At this session it was agreed by unanimous vote, save one, to send an initial letter to the Baptist Association, which, if the members of that body should be like-minded, might lead to continued correspondence. As that letter is of interest as showing the spirit of Christian comity held and exercised thus early by our fathers, a transcript of it, slightly abridged, is subjoined:

To the New Hampshire Association.

Dearly Beloved in the Lord:

Feeling our hearts expand with love for the world, and with complacency toward all, of every name and denomination, where we find the divine image, we hereby testify our prayer for your prosperity.

We wish that all shyness, evil surmising, evil thinking in any of your hearts, or our own, against our neighbors or brethren, may be forever expelled. Let us mutually lay aside every weight, and set the Lord, the worth of his cause, and immortal souls constantly before our eyes.

Our hearts and our doors have been, and still are, open to messengers of Jesus, of whatever name. We pray for and rejoice in the advancing reign of him who is King of kings and Lord of lords.

From your sincere friends of the Baptist Quarterly Meeting, held at New Durham, New Hampshire, June 3, 1786.

PELATIAH TINGLEY, *Clerk.*

Benjamin Randall

This letter speaks frankly, and yet manifests a kind, conciliatory spirit. It shows a desire that, while holding up the truth on either side, there be no feeling of acrimony or censoriousness, and that, while honestly holding some different sentiments, they fraternize so far as could be, in efforts to promote the cause which all Christians hold dear, the cause which has as its end the good of the world and the glory of God.

After a time an answer was received and another letter sent by the Quarterly Meeting. But, as neither was recorded, we can know nothing of their contents. Thus the correspondence ended. But thus it would not have been a hundred years later.

At the September session it was agreed to reaffirm a former vote on communion, that " It is proper to commune with one who, though not baptized by immersion, yet gives evidence of a change of heart, and daily leads a Christian life."

Near the close of the year, Mr. Randall traveled somewhat extensively in Maine,

Benjamin Randall

during which he attended some sixty meetings and saw many displays of God's grace. He says:

I met crowds flocking together from all directions; both by water and by land. I enjoyed great freedom in preaching Jesus, and had much success all along those islands of the sea

XVII

DURING the time covered by this chapter the young denomination under the leadership of Mr. Randall was steadily and healthily increasing. As had been hoped, the Quarterly Meeting system was working harmoniously. Its sessions had large attendance, and there was always good preaching and devout worship, and there radiated forth evangelistic influences which reached far into the country surrounding the localities that entertained the delegates. The sessions, with the quarterly letters to the churches, were educating the people in matters pertaining to union, doctrine, and usage.

With peace, plenty, equal rights, and just laws, what a paradise this world might be! But the golden age of such a state, if it is to be on earth, waits upon the slow widening

[123]

Benjamin Randall

of men's thoughts " with the process of the suns."

About the time under consideration a few cases of irregularity developed among the churches. Cases that should have been settled in churches where they originated, were, at this early period, taken to the Quarterly Meeting for adjustment. As illustrative of methods pursued in discipline by the early fathers, a few cases are given.

In a case of slight deflection, the offender was simply admonished. That being well received, and a promise given to amend, the matter dropped. In another case, David Young and family had accused Jeremiah Dow of certain criminal acts. In vindication, Dow had taken out a warrant for defamation against Young. Investigation proved the charges to be untrue. Settled, by having the accusing family severally confess, and the accused withdraw his warrant.

From several other methods of harmonizing discordant elements, but one is here selected, and that because it was found to

Benjamin Randall

be so effective that it was afterward frequently resorted to. It appears that Hibbard and Dunton, both good men, had a
case of difference which they regarded suf-
ficiently serious to be submitted to Quarterly
Meeting for settlement. After a statement
of the grievance before the conference,
Brother Coombs expressed a conviction that,
should the conference resolve itself into a
prayer-meeting, and commit the whole matter to God, he would soon restore harmony.
The conference did as Brother Coombs suggested, and results were as he prophesied.

Mr. Randall was very forbearing. He
had that charity which suffers long and is
kind. But he had withal high ideals as to
church consistency, and where persuasion
failed he could be stern in rebuke. In the
constituency of the early churches were
several former schoolmasters; and the majority agreed with them that good discipline
was an important factor of all good government; hence, where transgressors resisted
conciliatory efforts for their reform, the

purity of the church demanded extreme measures. After offenders had been dealt with according to scriptural methods, if they were still incorrigible they were regretfully but promptly excluded.

The establishment of a Quarterly Meeting emergency fund had been decided upon. At a later session the question was asked as to the manner of raising it. The laconic answer of the conference was, " By free contributions." This was simple and sure; so simple that some may at this time think it indicated a lack of ability to plan a complicated system of church finance. But if it be borne in mind that this was long before the invention of some devices now in vogue for raising church and benevolent funds, charitable allowance may be made.

We must admit that these people were a bit old-fashioned in their notions as to their proper relations to God and each other. They were pretty well acquainted with an old-fashioned Book, and its teachings probably colored their judgment. Maybe some

Benjamin Randall

of them remembered a call for offerings, and the response, as recorded in an old, old story, which runs thus: "And the Lord spake unto Moses, saying, Speak unto the children of Israel, that they bring me an offering: of every man that giveth it willingly with his heart ye shall take my offering. And they came, every one whose heart stirred him up, and every one whom his spirit made him willing, and they brought the Lord's offering to the work of the tabernacle of the congregation, and for all his service."

Whatever the source of inspiration, a respectable emergency fund was raised and sustained "by free contributions." That too, during years when our country was struggling through the most depressing financial experiences it has ever known. To anticipate, it may be said here that for many years, and until better civic and ecclesiastical government obtained, this fund did incalculable good, along lines first seen in vision by its founder, Benjamin Randall.

Benjamin Randall

In the early part of 1787, Mr. Randall made an extensive tour through the western section of New Hampshire. As usual, revivals attended his evangelistic efforts, which, in some cases, developed into churches, while elsewhere existent churches were strengthened by large additions.

During this period additions were made to the ministry by the ordination of Nathan Merrill and J. McCarson. At Bristol, Maine, twenty were baptized and a church organized. Buxton asked for the ordination of a candidate and admission to the Quarterly Meeting.

Mr. Randall closes his record for 1787 by a brief review and reflections suggested thereby. He entered this record:

I was rejoiced at hearing of the revival of religion all through the country, east and west. Blessed be the Lord! May all the messengers come like doves, each with an olive leaf. Great harmony has prevailed in the business transactions. Large numbers have been added to the churches

Benjamin Randall

The church at Weeks Corner, Maine, had for the first time invited the Quarterly Meeting. Notice had been sent to surrounding towns. Anticipation had been thoroughly aroused. With some there was probably a large element of curiosity. They had heard of a Free Baptist Quarterly Meeting and wanted to see what it was like. With many, as the sequel proved, there was a deep hungering and thirsting for spiritual betterment.

On the morning of the first day the people of that section looked out over a level of snow, below which fences and other landmarks had modestly sunk out of sight. The most prominent objects in view were the big drifts which blockaded all highways leading to Weeks Corner. Conditions in evidence answered in most respects to a description of New England given by a Southerner, who visited this country for the first time in midwinter. He said that what impressed him most was the piled-up condition of things here: " The hills were piled above

Benjamin Randall

the plains; the mountains above the hills;
the rocks above the mountains; the snow
above the rocks; the wind above the snow;
and cold above everything."

But those sturdy New Englanders were
not to be daunted by anything so trifling as
a snow-storm; the snow retarded, but did
not prevent, a large attendance. Churches
were well represented, reports were encouraging, business was disposed of with harmony and despatch, devotional meetings
were well sustained, and preaching was attended with much demonstration of divine
power.

Soon after the session got fairly under
way there were evidences of an approaching revival. Christians were moved to in-
tercessory prayer, and sinners began to confess their desire for salvation. The work
went on with much power till a goodly number from various parts of the town, and
beyond, were rejoicing over a new-born
hope. A transcript from Mr. Randall's journal is of interest here:

Benjamin Randall

The season seemed to me to be almost
heaven. While I was preaching from Ephe-
sians 4: 30, the power of God attended, a
great number were struck to the heart and
cried for mercy. Then, when I was preaching again from Hebrews 10 : 3, the same
was repeated. At communion the impress-
iveness was so great as to be almost unen-
durable. The house seemed much like being
full of angels. "Oh, come, magnify the
Lord with me, and let us exalt his name together!"

On the twenty-first of June, 1790, Mr.
Randall was summoned by a message to go
in haste to see his father at Ossipee, twenty-
two miles distant, in what proved to be the
last sickness. He reached the bedside just
in time to witness his father's departure.
Though too late to receive a final benedic-
tion, he was comforted by the remembrance
of the excellent life his parent had lived.
The remains were borne to New Durham on
a horse-litter. Impressive funeral services
were held at the house of Elder Randall,
who preached the sermon of the occasion

Benjamin Randall

from Psalm 37: 37: "Mark the perfect man, and behold the upright: for the end of that man is peace." Then the venerable form of Captain Randall, followed by a large and sympathetic procession, was laid to rest in the family burying-ground.

XVIII

THE year 1791 opened with Mr. Randall while he was wading through one of the most depressing experiences of his ministry. The expansion of the new denomination had exceeded the supply of ministerial help. Most of the churches were suffering for lack of pastoral care. Respecting the field covered by these churches it might be said, " The harvest truly is great, but the laborers are few." This scarcity of laborers was attributable, in part at least, to Mr. Randall's extreme caution in inducting men to the ministry. He had high ideals as to ministerial standards, and would " lay hands suddenly on no man."

To his humiliation and grief, the New Durham church, which was naturally regarded as an example by others of its association, was in such a state of spiritual disorder as to need what surgeons call "heroic treatment." The efforts put forth for reclaiming delinquents had in many cases proved of no avail. Hopeful of winning back this class, yet fearful of taking any steps that might result in driving them farther away, the pastor had borne and borne, till convinced that forbearance had ceased to be a virtue.

But what should be done? This was now the perplexing question. We of the present day, with our light from history since made, would say, Let the living members slough off the dead part and cast it away. That is, let a church discipline itself. If it has in its membership incorrigible offenders, exclude them. Meantime, let the church maintain its identity. This probably was the proper course for the New Durham church to take. This was in later years conceded by Mr. Randall as the best general rule, though it did not then suggest itself to him as the most feasible for that case.

Benjamin Randall

Whether wise or otherwise, this is the way he did it: after visiting his parish and thereby preparing the minds of his people, Mr. Randall announced a meeting at which decisive action would be taken. As the meeting had been widely advertised it had a large attendance. After stating the condition of the church and his fruitless efforts to correct its irregularities, Mr. Randall proceeded to say:

Therefore, considering how small is the number who stand fast in the truth, in comparison with those who have turned back, and that our covenant agreements are broken by the ungodly conduct of those professors who have become backslidden:

Agreed, that we now regard our church connections dissolved, and proclaim it so to the world. Also, that these doings be publicly read on the two next consecutive Sabbaths.

Then, as a number present felt their hearts warm toward each other, and wished to arise and covenant anew in church relationship, March twenty-third was appointed for all like-minded to meet for that purpose.

As the news of this action spread, it caused no little stir in the vicinity. Some blamed Mr. Randall, and some justified him for the move. On the day appointed a goodly number met, discussed ways and means of future procedure, and adjourned to April thirteenth. At this meeting twenty-one persons declared themselves in fellowship and were reorganized into a church.

These brethren once more started with a prospect of better order. All felt relieved and animated with new life. The first work to which they addressed themselves was in the line of reclaiming their delinquent brethren. Their efforts were successful only in part.

Mr. Randall seemed to have received a fresh baptism of the Holy Spirit, and more power attended his preaching, while the people flocked together with renewed eagerness to hear. Under his sermon of May eighth, conviction was manifested by a number.

Benjamin Randall

The next day some fifty became deeply affected and several cried for mercy. The revival thus started continued with power.
Meetings were held with success, for a time
almost every day and evening. Among
those who became trophies of grace were a
large number of the most influential and
promising young people of the town.

Mr. Randall had six baptismal services
within a few weeks, till sixty-seven were
added to the twenty-one members of the reorganized church, making a total of eighty-
eight. These accessions included John Buzzell, Simon Pottle, and Joseph Boody, all of
whom became ministers.

As John Buzzell was so intimately connected with the early history of our denomination, a few words of introduction may
here be admissible. A descendant from sterling English ancestry, John Buzzell opened
his eyes for the first time at Barrington,
New Hampshire, September 16, 1766. He
obtained a good education for the times,
taught several terms, and at the time of his

baptism was the New Durham schoolmaster. He had a well-developed physique, an imposing presence, and a good command of language. He at once began to preach the gospel of free grace, and was thenceforward one of Randall's ablest coworkers.

The June session of the Quarterly Meeting was, as usual, held at New Durham. Those from abroad soon caught the spirit of the place, and from the reflex influence the work at New Durham received a new impulse. The reports at this session were generally encouraging. New Durham was reported by Robert Oram, son of Elder Randall, thus:

The work of the Lord prospers among us. A most blessed union prevails. The Lord reigns. Glory to his blessed name!

A revival, begun in Middleton, had extended into Brookfield and Wakefield. This was under the labors of John Buzzell. The work commenced from his first sermon. His brother Aaron, who became such an efficient minister, was the first convert of this effort. Revivals were also reported at Kittery, Barrington, Bristol, and Raymond. Churches had been organized during the year at Kittery, Pittsfield, and Ossipee Hill.

Because of the pressing need of labor at home, Randall spent as little time as possible in his Kennebec tour this year. After his return, in a report of that tour, he says: " Experienced a wonderful display of God's power."

Thus the finger of God may scatter the darkest clouds, his hand make reverses stepping-stones to victory, and his blessing transmute trials into glory.

XIX

EXPERIENCE had taught Mr. Randall and his brethren that the denomination, in its expansion, had outgrown its representative arrangement entered into nine years before, in the Quarterly Meeting formation. It had become impossible for every church to report itself to every session of the body as the rule required.

Feeling the importance of a remedy, Randall introduced the matter to his home church, assembled May ninth, when the question was duly considered. He and seven others were chosen to meet delegates from all his other churches in New Hampshire, to devise some means of relief. Results were to be presented at the next Quarterly Meeting session, and to be adopted if there thought best.

Benjamin Randall

The proposed meeting was held May twenty-third, at the residence of James Lock, in Barnstead. It consisted of representatives from New Durham, Pittsfield, Middleton, and Barrington. It was agreed:

That the name of the present Quarterly Meeting, holding its annual sessions at New Durham, be changed to that of a Yearly Meeting.

That a new class of meetings, each to be held once in three months, be introduced between this and the churches, with the name of Quarterly Meetings.

That each church attend to all its local business, maintain good discipline, take the scriptural steps with delinquents, to the last admonition; then, if unsuccessful, refer the matter to the Quarterly Meeting. That each church, as now, have a clerk to keep its records, full and plain. That the church send its clerk to each session of the Quarterly Meeting, with his book of records, and several others as messengers. That through its clerk and messengers, each church report its condition to each session of the Quarterly Meeting.

Benjamin Randall

It was agreed that the messengers representing the several churches belonging thereto constitute the Quarterly Meeting potential. That the Quarterly Meeting hold its sessions at such times and places as agreed upon. That it have a clerk who shall keep a full and plain record of all doings, and transcribe in his book the records of the several churches. That the Quarterly Meeting adjust all difficulties that may be referred to it by the churches, or arise in its executive sessions, if able; but if not, refer the same to the Yearly Meeting.

That the Yearly Meeting consist of delegates from the several Quarterly Meetings, hold its sessions annually, at times and places agreed upon, adjust all matters referred to it by the Quarterly Meetings, and transact any other legitimate business. It shall devise ways and means for the welfare and efficiency of its constituency, and exercise a general supervision over the entire denomination.

The new system was unanimously adopted and was to go into operation at once, with Mr. Randall as recording secretary.

Benjamin Randall

It was also recommended that the same plan be adopted by the gatherings at Edgecomb, Gorham, and Parsonsfield, Maine. These recommendations were approved and adopted by these bodies.

This system provided that each church have a monthly meeting for the transaction of its local business; that several contiguous churches constitute a Quarterly Meeting; and that all the Quarterly Meetings covering a State, or other agreed-upon territory, combine for an annual session, to be called a Yearly Meeting.

This was the ideal. But it took several years of working the plan for the several bodies in the combination to learn their exact relative duties.

To meet the demands of new conditions, which arose from time to time, alterations, amendments, and supplements were demanded and made.

For more than fifty years, until the organization of General Conference, the Yearly Meeting was the highest ecclesiasti-

Benjamin Randall

cal court of the denomination. It served the purpose intended, and its decisions were respected by the people.

Thus far these organizations have been considered mostly from a business standpoint. But their sessions were of interest to the general public, mainly as centers of religious instruction and worship. Most of the business was done at side sessions, leaving much time for meetings of a purely religious nature. People came to these meetings from near and far, many of whom were hungering and thirsting for the gospel as proclaimed by the preachers of free grace. In confirmation of this statement, John Buzzell's testimony is instructive and interesting:

These meetings called the attention of thousands to hear the word of God who, perhaps, would have remained ignorant of these things if their attention had not been excited by these means. I have known persons of respectability to travel nearly twenty miles to attend a Monthly Meeting; and have seen

Benjamin Randall

as many as a hundred spectators at a church conference, when the church consisted of only ten members. At Quarterly Meetings I have often seen thousands flocking from different parts to hear the word. And when we have been under the necessity of repairing to groves for want of room, I have frequently seen them climb the trees, like Zacchæus, to see and hear, as it seemed, at the hazard of their lives. Yet I never knew a person to receive harm on such occasions.

Many who have come to these meetings have returned new creatures, praising God for redeeming love and saving grace.

The Yearly Meetings have also been attended with an equivalent blessing. Hundreds of souls that now belong to this denomination, and others, have located their first religious awakening in one of our Monthly, Quarterly, or Yearly Meetings.

Here we have an illustration, in part, of Mr. Buzzell's general statement. The scene was at a country town in Maine. The local church had invited the Yearly Meeting. They had raised and covered in a meeting-house of goodly proportions. They had laid

Benjamin Randall

loose, temporary floors, and fitted up rough-board seats for the occasion. Here they held the preliminary sessions and services. Here Mr. Randall preached the first sermon. But the coming multitude soon outgrew the capacity of the house. Here we will let one who constituted a part of that assembly finish the story; his language shows the impressive nature of the scene.

It was September: a beautiful Sabbath morning, the day of the great gathering of the new sect. Nature had just put on her brilliant attire, as if vying with man in worship to the Maker of all. My father, though not given to piety, consented to take all—mother, brothers, and sisters—to the spot where the public mind, as with one accord, seemed centering. Approaching with others, we entered a beautiful grove, and soon came to a widely extended ledge, of almost snowy whiteness. Upon this was erected a speaker's stand, with a table near, spread with communion service. The vessels were bright and glistening; the table coverings and napkins were as clean as the purest snow.

Benjamin Randall

The immense congregation, sitting around under the forest shade, were giving close attention to a sermon by Elder Tingley. I then, for the first time, saw Elder Randall, who was sitting upon the stand with other speakers. A heavenly glow seemed to rest on his countenance. How impressively did the whole scene strike my young heart, over which only thirteen summers had passed!

I had read of the crucified Saviour, wrapped in clean linen, and could hardly divest myself of the idea that the real body of Christ was lying upon that table before us, hidden from view only by those coverings, and that this was almost an exact representation of apostolic times.

As for the speaker, his manner was peculiar. He would strike the first of his sentence on a high key and drop to a lower on the latter part. He would comprehend much in a few words; but soon, how I wished him through, and that Randall would commence! In this I was at length gratified. And oh, how he spoke! burning words, right to the heart.

The impression then received by me can

Benjamin Randall

never be erased from the tablet of my memory. The influence was to change the entire habit of my thinking, to set me wholly upon a new course, and control my subsequent existence for good. I praise God for that day!

XX

A YOUNG man by the name of Dickey, gifted in prayer and exhortation, had gone from Epsom, New Hampshire, to Strafford, Vermont, there to remain awhile on business. Finding a general disregard of all things religious, he soon began to call on the people to turn from their sins and obey the commandments of God. These efforts were soon blessed by a gracious outpouring of God's spirit and the conversion of souls.

Calvinistic ministers soon visited the place, baptized whom they could, and organized a church. But Dickey was a Free Baptist. And from his representation of the new order, in the region from which he came, a number of the community desired to send for aid from that source. Hence the following letter:

[149]

Benjamin Randall

To the Baptist church of New Durham.

DEAR BRETHREN:

By agreement of a number of friends here, having a desire for the welfare of each other and for our fellow creatures, we now think it expedient, according to the light and manifestation of God's word, to come into church order of government, as the Scriptures direct. And being informed by Brother Dickey of your standing and order, these being agreeable to our minds, we request some of the elders of your church to come, as soon as possible, to our assistance. For we are alone, as to sentiment, in this part of the country.

From your friend and brother,

SAMUEL RICH.

STRAFFORD, VERMONT,
September 10, 1771.

The New Durham brethren regarded this as another Macedonian call, but were then forced to answer that, as their pastor had just returned from a journey of a hundred and sixty miles east, and must go again in two weeks on important business to Waterboro, Maine, and then attend to other engagements, they could not comply with their request till another season.

So, on July 25, 1792, Elder Randall, with John Buzzell as companion, bearing the commendation of the church, set off on the proposed mission. On arrival, Mr. Randall preached a number of times to the people, with great freedom.

The people were found to be of mixed sentiments, but all so absorbed in the overflowing joys of their new love that points of doctrine held a subordinate place in their regards. They would not harbor the idea of being separated and being formed into two different societies. For a time the question was most anxiously considered among them, about the direction in which they would move. Meantime, they were left to their own volition.

Finally, at a meeting held August first, having, as they said, duly considered the matter, those already formed into a church concluded to alter their Articles of Faith so far

Benjamin Randall

as to take a stand with their Free Baptist brethren. Accordingly, however much Mr. Randall might have feared from their previous differing views, he extended to them the hand of fellowship.

The day before he had baptized Jacob Hadley and Daniel Hadley, of Tunbridge, an adjoining town. Nathaniel Brown was one of this organization. He was a young man of early promise, which he later fulfilled. After successful evangelistic work in Vermont, he was the first minister to preach the gospel of free grace in western New York, where he organized the Bethany church and, indirectly, the Genesee Quarterly Meeting, and the Holland Purchase Yearly Meeting.

Randall and Buzzell returned by the way of Salisbury, New Hampshire, where, by invitation, they held a few religious services. As one of the immediate results, a glorious work of grace began. But they were obliged to turn away and leave the work in the hands of another denomination.

Benjamin Randall

This tour of about two weeks was attended with much sacrifice and suffering on the part of those missionaries. The roads were bad and much of the way through extended forests. Many times, as night overtook them, they had no better place to sleep than the bare floor of one of the log cabins which were sparsely scattered along the way. The weather was hot and sultry. The distance traveled was about three hundred miles. Before they reached the end of their journey, riding became very distressing.

When they were about to separate, Mr. Randall presented his companion two of the four pistareens, which represented the sum-total of their money receipts while absent. A pistareen was a small Spanish silver coin, valued in the United States at about seventeen cents. Buzzell refused the offer; but Randall thrust the bits into his hand, saying, " You shall take them! Carry them to your wife! "

This case of home mission work has been

Benjamin Randall

given somewhat in detail; not that, as considered in connection with the general pioneer work of the times, it is exceptional, but as illustrative of experiences common to those early evangelists, records of which in most cases never found their way to public recognition.

XXI

THE year 1792 was nearing its close. The months already past had been crowded with events of importance to Mr. Randall and the cause he represented. But before the year was allowed to join the receding procession, other important events were added to the record.

A council duly authorized met at Wolfeboro, October nineteenth, and organized a Free Baptist church, the first church of any kind organized in the town. The covenant, in Mr. Randall's handwriting, is still extant. Four days later a council, consisting of Randall, Weeks, and Whitney, met at Middleton to examine, with reference to ordination, John Buzzell and Isaac Townsend.

As intimated in a former chapter, our fathers were cautious about inducting men

[155]

Benjamin Randall

into the ministry. Whatever the natural or acquired abilities of candidates, certain conditions were indispensable. The men must be of good repute, mentally balanced, and deeply pious. They must be sound in biblical doctrines according to evangelical interpretation, have aptness to teach and ability to edify, have a gift for soul-winning, give evidence of a divine call; and, withal, the more education they had received the better. One of the ordeals through which a candidate usually had to pass was the preaching of a trial sermon.

Now, respecting the cases under consideration, the following items are gleaned from an old record: They first had worship at the Middleton meeting-house, where Buzzell preached on trial to good acceptance. The council then repaired to a private house. Buzzell proceeded to give an account of his conversion, call to the ministry, and success in former efforts at soul-winning. Then followed critical questions by the brethren on the council, and all to good satisfaction.

REV. JOHN BUZZELL
A typical Free Baptist minister of the Randallian period

Benjamin Randall

Townsend was put through a similar course, except the trial sermon, and with like results. It was agreed that Buzzell be ordained at the meeting-house the following day, and that Townsend be ordained the day after at Wolfeboro. Randall, Weeks, Whitney, and Boody were selected to conduct the services.

Here it may be admissible to turn a sidelight on some ordination customs—or perhaps, more properly speaking, accessories—peculiar to the times. In those early days a really orthodox ordination was held to be an affair in which the rabble must have a part as well as the church and the council.

The people from a wide area would assemble. A procession would be formed, sometimes headed by a band of music, to escort the pastor-elect and other dignitaries from some public place to the meeting-house. And while the services would be in process there, drinking, horse-swapping, and general carousing would be the order (?) without. The day would end with public festivities, at which strong drink would be a considerable part of the entertainment.

The expense of all this would be paid from the public chest. A work called "Buxton Centennial" gives a few illustrative statements. Under date of 1762, the record runs thus: "Twenty pounds"—about one hundred dollars—"lawful money was voted to defray the charges of ordaining Mr. Paul Coffin." In the same account, farther on, we have this: "A very plentiful entertainment for the council and strangers was provided at the expense of the proprietors."

Though no parade, public dinner, music, or rum was offered in connection with the ordination of Mr. Buzzell, by common impulse a mixed multitude gathered for the occasion; the better class to witness, if possible, the services, and the baser for carousal.

At ten o'clock in the morning about one thousand people gathered in and about the house of God to witness the interesting and impressive ceremonies; while about another

Benjamin Randall

thousand were out by themselves to spend the day in revelry.

Elder Randall preached the sermon from 2 Corinthians 5 : 20: "Now then we are ambassadors for Christ." Weeks offered the prayer of consecration and gave the charge. Whitney gave the hand of fellowship, and Boody offered the closing prayer. The sermon was well adapted to the occasion, and was delivered with demonstration of the Spirit and with power. Each part of the services was well sustained. The whole was solemn and impressive. It was a day of good to God's people, notwithstanding the annoyance of the rabble.

In accordance with previous arrangements, the next day the same council met at Wolfeboro and ordained Isaac Townsend as pastor of the Free Baptist church there.

At a legal meeting the town of Wolfeboro, after having organized a church of eight members, had voted to settle Mr. Ebenezer Allen as its minister, and arranged for his ordination to occur on the same day

Benjamin Randall

appointed for that of Mr. Townsend. The evident intent of this was that Townsend should not be the first minister ordained in the town, thereby entitling him to the town land.

Previous to the ordination of Mr. Allen a remonstrance had been signed by eighteen citizens and presented to the town authorities, protesting against the move and declaring that they would not pay any minister-tax to the town, as they were accustomed to attend the other church.

The usual rabble was in evidence, as was their manner, at the town gathering. At the Townsend ordination the assembly was large, orderly, and respectful. It was a day of great good to the locality and the regions beyond.

Let us be thankful that, by common consent, such religious rivalry has long since disappeared, and that not only religious tolerance, but a spirit of mutual helpfulness now dominates all Christian bodies.

XXII

CHURCH MUSIC—CONGREGATION VERSUS CHOIR
1793

DURING the eighteenth century most
of the church singing was congregational. A record of it contains this, " They
sang with decorum if not ability." But
some daring innovators emphasized the importance of " ability " withal, and suggested
that church music might be improved by
giving the whole matter over to the exclu-
sive management of a few trained singers.
This suggestion met with scant favor among
New England churches, and in some cases it
was stoutly antagonized.

The suggestion for these improvements
(?) reached New Durham during the year
of grace 1793. It appears that a number
in the town had given attention to the rules
of singing, and had formed themselves into

M   [161]

Benjamin Randall

an association called " The Singing Society." At length the leader wrote to Mr. Randall, requesting that choir singing be introduced into the Sabbath services of the church, and that they be permitted to conduct that part of worship. From the first our people had given to sacred song a large place in their worship. Their aversion to surrendering that service to the monopoly of a choir was expressed in Mr. Randall's response, portions of which are subjoined:

NEW DURHAM, May 10, 1793.
Mr. Jackson and The Singing Society.

In response to your request, we would say:

As " God is a Spirit, and they that worship him must worship him in spirit and in truth," nothing but spiritual service can be pleasing to him. Hence, should a society, ever so large, and understanding the rules of music ever so well, render the service of song without the spirit, it could only please the ear of men, and not the great heart-searching God, who requireth truth in the inward parts.

[162]

Benjamin Randall

You well say that singing is a part of the worship of God, and ought to be performed with sincerity. Just so. Such is the declaration of the Scriptures: " I will pray with the spirit, and I will pray with the understanding also: I will sing with the spirit, and I will sing with the understanding." " Let the word of Christ dwell in you richly in all wisdom; teaching and admonishing one another in psalms and hymns and spiritual songs, singing with grace in your hearts to the Lord." " Speaking to yourselves in psalms and hymns and spiritual songs, singing and making melody in your heart to the Lord."

How important that we sing with the spirit! How presumptuous must it be for any one who lives after a vain and carnal manner, or uses his tongue in profane language, to attempt to lead an important part of the solemn worship of God! As well may an unconverted man lead in prayer or preaching as in singing. For the latter is equally sacred with the former.

But to conclude. We wish you well. May you all be engaged to know God! May you all come into that state in which you

Benjamin Randall

can worship him in spirit and truth here, and be prepared to join with the millions of worshipers hereafter.

Yet, we must inform you that, for reasons above stated, we believe it cannot be pleasing to God for us to give our consent for his worship to be led by any but those who are practical believers in Christ.

In behalf of the church at New Durham,

BENJAMIN RANDALL, *Pastor.*

Here it should be observed that Mr. Randall did not object to the regulation of church music by rule, but to monopoly of it by the unconverted.

Now, we are in sympathy with both Mr. Randall and the leader of "The Singing Society." The position of Mr. Randall, that the entire congregation should have the opportunity of worship by song, is sustained by the sacred Scriptures, the usages of the early Christian church, and of all churches ever since, at seasons of their deepest piety and greatest efficiency.

In order that singing be with the under-

Benjamin Randall

standing as well as with the spirit, it must be
regulated by rules. Henry Ward Beecher,
in one of his Yale lectures, speaking of
church music, said: "A choir is necessary
to have the best kind of congregational singing." He would have the organ and the
choir lead and regulate the music, while
"all the people" have opportunity to worship in song, measuring up to right standards according to their several ability. And
that is the way they did it, as we happen to
know by personal acquaintance with both
Mr. Beecher and his Free Baptist chorister.
In that same Yale lecture, Mr. Beecher had
the modesty to say: "It is the singing which
draws the people to Plymouth church, not
the preaching."

It is a well-known fact that Mr. Spurgeon had simply a musical director to lead
his three or four thousand hearty English
:and Welsh worshipers in sacred song. As
to the effect, we have it from those who have
attended the Tabernacle services that it was
indescribably impressive and grand.

XXIII

ON THE TRAIL OF THE PIONEER
1793-1797

EARLY in the history of the colonies the District of Maine—as it was then called, because under the government of Massachusetts—offered special land-grant inducements to settlers. These were accepted by hundreds and thousands of home-seekers. The first settlers were mostly from Massachusetts, and descendants of the Puritans. While with these people some of the hard Puritanic features had been softened, they retained the physical robustness, mental vigor, and religious tendencies of their noble ancestors. As a rule, they were law-abiding citizens, reared large families, established good schools, and welcomed the church.

They first took possession of the many islands and extended seacoast lands. Then

Benjamin Randall

they followed the rivers and smaller streams to the interior. From thence they ramified into the unbroken forests.

Their mode of transporting their families and goods was by sailing craft to the islands and coastlands, and as far as possible up the rivers. Overland they proceeded on foot, on horseback, on packhorses, and on ox-teams. These were always interesting experiences, and sometimes a bit of romance was associated with these pioneer movements.

One young man, after helping Washington gain the liberty of the colonies, took up a claim in the Maine woods, made a clearing, built a log cabin, and then returned to Massachusetts for his wife and babe. These he placed in the saddle of his horse and packed their scanty belongings behind, while he, with gun in hand and his faithful dog at his side, marched ahead. On leaving the road they took an Indian trail for a few miles, thence were guided by blazed trees to their new home.

Benjamin Randall

Mr. Francis Tufts came from Nobleboro, Massachusetts, moving his goods and family on horseback. His children were carried in panniers made of basket stuff. They followed up the Kennebec to Sandy River. Thence they took to the woods, being guided the last day by blazed trees.

Later Mr. Tufts went to Boston with two others, and purchased of the commonwealth of Massachusetts, for themselves and others, the entire township of Farmington for four hundred pounds, about two thousand dollars. His position in society gave him a wide and controlling influence, which he used for civic righteousness and religion.

In many respects the case of Mr. John F. Woods was similar to that of Mr. Tufts. Mr. Woods came from Dunstable, with an ox-team, being twenty-three days on the road. He also was a leading citizen of the town. These men were not only pioneer settlers, but pioneer Christians and founders of Free Baptist churches in the Sandy River valley.

[168]

Benjamin Randall

The pioneer preachers made many sacrifices and suffered great hardships in connection with their work among the early settlers. The case of Rev. Samuel Weeks is illustrative. One of Mr. Randall's strongest colaborers, he was not only successful as an evangelist, but as a founder of churches. A native of Greenland, New Hampshire, he began preaching at Gilmanton, and later moved to Parsonsfield, Maine.

The surrounding country was then mostly a wilderness. One day in January, 1795, Weeks made his way through the woods, guided by blazed trees, to Porter, to attend an evening meeting. On his return, as he was crossing a branch of the Ossipee River, the ice gave way, and he fell from his horse into the water. Confused by this accident, and the night being very dark, he lost his path and could not find the spotted trees which would guide him.

Weeks wandered about for a while, calling, but in vain, for help. Not daring to proceed in any direction for fear of becom-

Benjamin Randall

ing lost, he decided to wait where he was till morning. Soon his clothes were frozen. Intense suffering was at length followed by numbness, accompanied by drowsiness. He knew that yielding to this stupor would lead to the sleep of death. So, by walking forth and back, rolling in the snow, and occasionally leaning against a tree to rest, he struggled desperately to drive off the almost overpowering desire to sleep, and succeeded in keeping awake.

When morning dawned, Mr. Weeks found his way to a house, and was carried home. Examination revealed the fact that his feet were so badly frozen as to require the amputation of portions of each foot. But sadder still, the shock broke down his nervous system, clouded his mind, and incapacitated him for public ministrations. The remaining thirty-seven years of his life were mostly spent in reading his Bible and in religious conversation with those who visited him. Thus, as a pioneer evangelist, he literally presented his body a living sacrifice to God.

Benjamin Randall

Many other examples might be given, quite as illustrative as the foregoing, of sacrifices made and hardships borne by Free Baptist ministers in their efforts to reach the early settlers of New England, the Middle States, and the great West. But here it must suffice to say that, to the remotest forest home, these evangelists followed the trail of the pioneer with the gospel of free grace.

Respecting New England, Mr. Randall's journal shows that he was the pioneer evangelist to all sections of country here mentioned, and beyond. Among other results of these efforts, churches sprang up in many places, and in some communities nearly every family became confessedly Christian.

As a source of cheer and encouragement to Mr. Randall, God gave him the satisfaction of seeing that the cause to which he had devoted his life was making real, substantial advancement in all parts of his wide parish. This was apparent, not only in numbers, but also in public standing. The doctrines he

Benjamin Randall

held and taught were finding acceptance with the more intelligent classes.

Another source of encouragement was the fact that a better-furnished ministry was developing—a ministry more capable of declaring their faith and more efficient in defending it. All these conditions were accepted by Mr. Randall as comforting assurances that God was directing his movements and leading **from victory to victory.**

XXIV

IN a former chapter mention was made of
the fact that the sessions of Free Baptist
assemblies of all kinds had large attendance.
As time passed these assemblies became more
and more centers of public interest, and
their sessions had corresponding attendance. But we desire here to speak more
especially of the New Hampshire Yearly
Meeting.

During the early years this body held its
regular sessions at New Durham. The time
selected was that part of June when the
forests had just put on their summer robes,
and all nature was on its best behavior.
After the enforced confinement of winter
and the bustle of " spring work " were over,
almost everybody in rural New Hampshire

Benjamin Randall

wanted to go somewhere. And, at the time of the Yearly Meeting, representatives of many parts of the State, and persons from beyond, aggregating hundreds, and in some cases thousands, set their faces toward New Durham. There were generally many from Portsmouth, and on one occasion six carriage-loads from Boston. At several sessions the Sunday congregations were estimated to be three thousand. Facts show that most of these pilgrims were actuated by higher motives than simply to enjoy a pleasant outing or to satisfy the cravings of an idle curiosity.

An article by the author, published a few years ago, contains a paragraph which so completely fits conditions under description that the substance of it is here reproduced.

If we should theorize we might say that, as these meetings were held before railroad service, at a time when carriages were the luxury of the few and most country roads were crude, it is improbable that three thousand people should assemble on a high hill, remote from common centers, to attend a religious meeting.

But here facts are more convincing than theories. Other religious bodies were busy expounding the decrees of God and making good on various lines of Christian work. Meanwhile, the great middle classes of New England were waking to the consciousness of a deep soul-hunger. As to no other body of Christians at that time, the Master was saying to his Free Baptist disciples, " Give ye them to eat." They obeyed the message, and the common people gladly received the Bread of Life at their hands, and were willing to make the necessary sacrifice to reach the assemblies where it was offered.

Another fact should here have consideration. Many had saddle-horses and some had carriages. Those thus provided could travel long distances with comparative ease. But those who had neither were accustomed to walk over space between them and the object of their interest, whatever that might be. So walking was not then regarded as

Benjamin Randall

the hardship that it has been since the general introduction of easier methods of travel. As to those who took long-distance walks to attend sessions of the New Hampshire Yearly Meeting, only a few can here have mention.

A company of pious women in Kittery and vicinity were accustomed to make an annual pilgrimage on foot to these meetings. This was to them a journey of two days each way. Jonathan Woodman, when a youth of eighteen years, walked from Sutton, Vermont, to Parsonsfield, Maine, to attend a Yearly Meeting. Mrs. Hannah Thorn several times walked from Lewiston to Westport, Maine, thirty-five miles each way, to attend a Yearly Meeting. Mrs. Joanna Horne many times walked forty miles, from her home in Moultonboro, to attend sessions of the Yearly Meeting held in Dover.

As the different processions of pilgrims joined each other at highway junctions, they would sometimes, as they neared the place of meeting, aggregate hundreds in line. The surrounding forests would echo with their songs of devotion. And the people no more needed hymn-books than did the birds that responded from the overhanging branches.

But how could the people of the town accommodate so many? The largest assembly was on the Sabbath, and at the close of the afternoon service many would start homeward. Yet enough would remain to make it a question requiring no small labor and outlay to answer practically. Some would entertain forty; some, sixty; some, eighty, and even more. For lodging they would assign separate rooms to men and women. They would part their beds and bedding, spread it out on the floors, and then, soldier-like, they would lie down in long rows. Whoever could enjoy the luxury of a blanket between him and the boards might regard himself fortunate.

One New Durham man of considerable property, with a large house and a heart to match, was a regular host on Yearly Meeting occasions. In after years his wife would

Benjamin Randall

relate some of her experiences as hostess. On such occasions, after furnishing her guests with every available article of softness in the house to lie upon, her only place for rest would be the bare floor of the attic. There she would seek a few hours' repose, but at one or two o'clock in the morning she would be astir again, preparing supplies for the table.

Now that we have heard the testimony of the hostess, the story of one of her guests may be of interest. A prominent minister of the denomination, then a young man recently converted, says:

On reaching Yearly Meeting, I put up at Esquire Runnels' with over one hundred others. When arrangements were made for the first night's lodging, the floors were completely covered, leaving me to get all the sleep I could sitting upon a block in the chimney-corner. As to stillness, there wasn't any. The house did not cease to echo with the voice of singing, prayer, or private conversation till morning called us to our new-day duties.

Benjamin Randall

Enjoying (?) for a while a similar entertainment the second night, I resorted to the dooryard where the wagons were, for lodgment in one of them. Putting my hand into the first, it fell on the face of a man in sound sleep; and so on to others. Despairing of success here, I returned to my block throne, to spend the remainder of the night as best I could. But the third night, going several miles out of the place, I found opportunity for repose.

In providing for horses, the brethren would sometimes hire a large pasture nearby, and keep it unfed till meeting-time, when it would be ready to afford the animals very good fare. Some, after filling their own pastures, would turn horses into their mowing fields, to find them completely fed down when meeting closed. On all such occasions the house, barn, and fields of Mr. Randall were laid under tribute to the fullest extent of their capacity.

Thus the people of New Durham, all through these early years, contributed largely to the support and development of

Benjamin Randall

the Free Baptist cause. Inspired by the
spirit and example of a leader wholly baptized into the work, they extended this hos-
pitality freely, gladly, and " heartily, as to
the Lord."

XXV

THE TRANSIT OF THE CENTURY
1799-1801

THE closing years of the eighteenth century and the opening years of the nineteenth were among the busiest years of Mr. Randall's very active career.

Certain people in Marshfield, Massachusetts, having applied to the Quarterly Meeting for a messenger to visit them and explain to them more fully the doctrines held and taught by Free Baptists, the request was referred to the New Durham church, and Mr. Randall was appointed to answer the call.

With Nathan Keniston as traveling companion, Mr. Randall started on this journey February twenty-sixth. On his arrival he was given a cordial reception. He there found open doors for meetings and open hearts for the gospel of free grace. On this

[181]

Benjamin Randall

circuit he took in Boston, Andover, Braintree, and Scituate. He was absent from home nearly a month, preached twenty-four times, and conducted many devotional meetings. A record in his journal runs thus: "All seemed to receive the gospel of free grace gladly, and many sinners were converted."

In the early March of 1800, Mr. Randall went on a missionary tour through western Vermont, where he found the work spreading gloriously under the evangelistic labors of Joseph Boody, Jr., of New Durham. In the previous June, in response to earnest invitations of friends and the promptings of duty, Boody went on an evangelistic tour through those regions. He preached at Hardwick, Greensboro, Hyde Park, Cabot, Danville, Dewey Gore, Wolcott, and Walden. He saw extensive revivals in all these towns. He had collected a company of fifty-two converts in Hardwick. These Mr. Randall embodied into a church. Others were gathered later. These towns were in

the region of Mr. Randall's visit. In all this
tour he enjoyed precious manifestations of
the Holy Spirit in connection with his
preaching.

At the June Yearly Meeting, held as usual
at New Durham, before the preliminary
business had been completed, the glory of
God came down in Pentecostal showers; so
that nothing could be done but adjourn business till Monday and attend worship.

This session entertained a request from
churches in Vermont to be organized into a
Quarterly Meeting. Elders Aaron Buzzell,
Daniel Lord, and John Shepard were constituted a council with discretionary power to
respond. A little later the Strafford Quarterly Meeting, Vermont, was received. In
this were five churches—Strafford, Tunbridge, Vershire, Corinth, and Brookfield,
which reported five ordained ministers and
three hundred and thirty members, and
added the pleasing statement that " the work
of God is gloriously spreading in all these
regions."

Benjamin Randall

Mr. Randall made his second visit to Marshfield and vicinity in August. He was gone seventeen days, visited much, and held about one religious service, on an average, each day of his absence.

Early in September he started on another extended tour in Maine. One dark night he lost his way in a dense forest. His horse broke through a bridge and both were precipitated down a steep bank. But as they fell upon a bed of thick bushes, both were rescued without serious injury to either. These experiences, though sad at the time, were reckoned among the sufferings which were not worthy to be compared with the glory revealed in preaching the gospel for the salvation of men.

He was away from home on this journey thirty-three days, attended sixty-one meetings, and traveled five hundred and seventy-four miles.

One incident illustrative of Mr. Randall's total-abstinence principles must stand for the many that cannot be admitted.

Benjamin Randall

On an afternoon of December, 1800, he left home, purposing to preach the next day at Alton; but when about two miles away he was attacked with a violent colic, an illness to which he was an occasional victim. He stopped at a Mrs. Willey's, where, for twelve hours, he struggled with excruciating pain. At times it was feared he must die. But, by the skill of his physician and the blessing of God, in a few days he was able to be carried home.

While he was suffering the most acute paroxysms of pain, it was suggested that if he would drink some liquor he might obtain relief. But he positively refused. Whereupon a bystander exclaimed: " I believe that these spells are sent upon Elder Randall as a judgment, because he is so bitterly opposed to using ardent spirits."

This incident illustrates at once the current opinion of the times respecting the use of liquors, and Mr. Randall's position on the subject. In this he was as much in advance of his times as he was on matters

[185]

religious. His rebukes of the drinking custom of his times were frequent and scathing.

Monday, May 18, 1801, found Mr. Randall on his way to New Hampton, where the Quarterly Meeting was to convene. " In the evening we held a meeting in Gilmanton— a blessed, powerful season." The next day, with a company of about forty, he took dinner at Brother Samuel Crockett's, in Meredith. In their host and family they found Christians with large hearts, keeping open doors for all of God's people.

Having been well refreshed with material sustenance, and the sweet opportunity for song and prayer, in the afternoon they moved on in order, two abreast, to the home of Deacon Pease, where another company was gathered in worship, led by Elder Martin. Because of this accession to their numbers, the company had to repair to the orchard for worship. This is reported as " a wonderful, very wonderful meeting."

On Wednesday morning the company set

Benjamin Randall

off again in double file, now a cavalcade of a hundred people on horseback, with Randall in the van. Among those who made up this procession of Christians were many excellent singers. When nearing the church edifice, where the crowd had already gathered, the cavalcade commenced a most solemn and impressive hymn. "And as the melodious strains from those voices floated out on the air, the effect was perfectly thrilling, not only to those singing, but to the waiting assembly."

At the meeting the devotional fervidness soon rose to such a point that many sinners began to pray for mercy. The scene was a fitting prelude to what was to follow. In business all gave excellent attention, though about six hundred were present.

Conference met for business the next morning, but for two hours or more there was no room for business. The religious fervidness had risen to such a high pitch that it seemed best to allow its expression in devotion and worship. In the afternoon,

Benjamin Randall

Elder Martin preached to the edification of all. Others followed with exhortation. Then the Lord's Supper was administered. "A powerful scene! Indescribably glorious! We had never witnessed such a Quarterly Meeting as this before."

The new century dawned upon general prosperity along all lines of Free Baptist activities. From sweeping revivals nearly all the churches were able to report accessions, and several new churches had been organized.

XXVI

FOR nearly a quarter of a century Mr. Randall had been engaged in building up churches, and to all his organizations, of whatever class, he had applied simply the name Baptist. Thus he gave testimony to the world that he was not laboring to bring out a separate denomination. He held himself as ever, acting within the bounds of the great Baptist family, to which family he had at all times maintained a perfectly loyal attitude, and in which he still claimed a home. And why not? Ever after receiving baptism at the hands of Rev. Mr. Hooper, he had lived true to Baptist principles. Nowhere had he swerved from them in the least degree. Hence, on Baptist grounds, he had as clear a title to the family name, shield, and prestige as the strictest of the strict.

Benjamin Randall

But, to the regret of Mr. Randall, it seemed that the time had come when it was best for him and his adherents to be known to the world by a distinguishing name. The following legislative act shows the epithet they accepted:

STATE OF NEW HAMPSHIRE.

In the House of Representatives, December 7, 1804.

Resolved, That the people in this State, known by the name of the Freewill Antipedobaptist Church and Society, shall be considered as a distinct religious sect or denomination, with all the privileges as such, of the constitution.

Sent up for concurrence,

JOHN LANGDON, *Speaker.*

In the Senate, December 8.

NICHOLAS GILMAN, *President.*

Not approved nor returned by His Excellency, the Governor, it therefore becomes a law.

JOSEPH PEARSONS, *Secretary of State.*

[190]

Benjamin Randall

It was reported by some of his friends that the governor excused himself from signing the resolution on the ground that, in his view, it was needless; that the Society possessed all the rights and immunities before that they could have after its passage; that by the constitution every religious sect in the State really stood on the same footing.

This view of the governor may have been the correct one; that is, as far as related to the period after the adoption of the constitution. Still, the resolution even in that case was of great importance, in that it tended to set things in a clear and unmistakable light. If the dominant sect for these long years had not really possessed any legal advantage over others, through a lack of proper understanding among the people or for some other cause, this sect had always succeeded in keeping alive the contrary sentiment.

There prevailed an impression that in a town provided with a minister of the Standing Order, a resident who never attended the meetings had to be fortified with a certificate

Benjamin Randall

of membership in another religious body or of adherence to it, in order to avoid being distrained upon for a tax to support that minister.

From this sentiment arose the fact that here and there town officers would ignore those certificates and levy upon the possessor, who would usually pay the tax rather than stand a lawsuit. One historian, referring to these conditions, says:

Indeed, these annoyances were numerous and grievous, far more so than those that roused our Revolutionary fathers to cut loose from the mother country.

The adoption of the resolution mentioned above resulted in no little advantage to the cause of our people, securing as it did to our denomination in the State a recognized legal standing by the side of the dominant sect, and sweeping away the last vestige of that religious oppression, against which Mr. Randall had been so valiantly contending ever since he commenced his ministry.

Benjamin Randall

Our people in Maine, and other religious bodies in this State, soon obtained like recognition. But to Mr. Randall belongs the credit of having been the pioneer in this contest for religious liberty.

As to the name under which we obtained State recognition, the second prefix soon fell into disuse. As " Baptist " was a synonym for immersed believers *only*, the word " Antipedo " was soon discovered to be superfluous, and was dropped—dropped before it ever got into our literature. As our people believed not only in free will, but in free grace and open communion as well, " will " came to be regarded as superfluous and also restrictive. So this word also was dropped, and left us only Free Baptists.

In the statement of the Baptist Brotherhood, agreed upon by representatives of the Baptist and Free Baptist denominations, in a meeting held in Brooklyn, New York, November, 1905, among many fraternal expressions, we find the following:

o

Benjamin Randall

In view of these facts, patent to all students of the situation, and moved by a spirit of fraternity, which is affecting the whole Christian world, both denominations, by an impulse unpremeditated on the human side, sought conference on the subject of reuniting the work. It seemed to many that both the letter and the spirit of Christian brotherhood called for the abandonment of divisions in the body of Christ, which have so little to justify and so much to rebuke them.

On recommendation of the joint committees, which met in Brooklyn, in November, 1905, the following resolution was approved by each of the Baptist Societies in their meetings at Washington, in May, 1907:

Resolved, That the Baptists and Free Baptists are so closely related by a history which long was common, and has always been kindred, that they enjoy closer fellowship and greater similarity in genius and spirit than are common between two Christian bodies. It is recognized as a fact that the original occasion and cause of separation between our two bodies have practically dis-

Benjamin Randall

appeared, and that in all essentials of Christian doctrine, as well as of church administration and polity, we are substantially one.

To this platform of accord was added by a joint committee, representing all of the agreeing Societies, met in Boston, Massachusetts, March 28, 1908, the following statement:

Differences, if still existing, may be left, where the New Testament leaves them, to the teaching of the Scriptures under the guidance of the Holy Spirit.

These joint committees have anticipated a transition period. During that period we are informed that:

The basis of union, and the action accompanying it, take a broad and liberal attitude toward names. These names are suggested as of equal validity: Baptist, Free Baptist, and United Baptist. One is as good as another. They may be used interchangeably. Either may include the other. We may continue to call ourselves Free Baptists

Benjamin Randall

and still be in the fellowship and the fold;
we may term ourselves United Baptists without ceasing to be either Baptists or Free
Baptists; we may use the name Baptist and
still be Free Baptists. In names no rigid
conformity is required.

The wisdom and grace that dominated
these joint committees are evinced in the
use of names suggested for this transition
period. But are not all these qualifying
terms burdens to be dropped as soon as
compatible with the safeguarding of pending
interests?

As Free Baptists, may we not consistently
hold to the simple name that Randall loved
and honored for the first quarter of a century of his public ministry? He regretfully
accepted a prefix as a necessity. We have
carried it for a hundred and ten years. But
if "it is recognized as a fact that the
original occasion and cause of separation
between our two bodies has practically disappeared," may we not now gratefully accept the magnanimity of our brethren of the

Benjamin Randall

larger body, soon drop our distinctive prefix, and call ourselves, what in heart we
really are, simply Baptists?

Of Washington it has been said: " The
name needs no prefix. Let it stand in its
simple grandeur. No other name can find
a fitting place beside it."

Of Baptist it may be said: The name
stands as an exponent of government of the
people, by the people, for the people. It
stands for a correctly interpreted Bible, a
regenerated membership, and a world-wide
evangelization. " The name needs no prefix. Let it stand in its simple grandeur.
No other name can find a fitting place beside
it."

XXVII

FAINT YET PURSUING
1807

THE opening of this year found Mr. Randall at home, sick, suffering, and unable to dress himself. But he soon rallied so far as to be able, with assistance, to conduct religious services near home and even beyond.

The January Quarterly Meeting was held at Sutton. Mr. Randall attended and reported "a melting season at the opening," the spirit of which characterized the entire session. General prosperity was reported from all sections. Ashby, Weare, and York churches were received.

On the second of February Mr. Randall, accompanied by his son William, started for the Yearly Meeting at Sandy River, Maine. He preached at several places on the way, also at the session and on his homeward journey. He was known through all the region of his journey, and people everywhere flocked to greet and hear him. On this journey he encountered cold, deep drifts, storms, and floods; yet he reached home in safety after eighteen days.

The next four months he spent almost exclusively in visiting various parts of New Hampshire, though most of the time so feeble that all movements were made with difficulty and attended with pain.

On the twenty-seventh of July, under a burning sun, he set out to attend the ordination of Stephen Gibson, at Ashby, Massachusetts, and reached his destination five days later. At the ordination, though he had been much weakened by hemorrhages from the lungs, he preached the sermon, offered the prayer of consecration, and gave the charge. It was an impressive occasion. The next day rain prevented a homeward start. In the evening Otis preached, and Randall spoke awhile, giving an appropriate parting message.

Benjamin Randall

Returning, Mr. Randall passed through Derryfield, where he visited General Stark, of Revolutionary fame. In his account of the interview, Mr. Randall wrote: "Had much interesting conversation." In this, probably, Revolutionary experiences in which both had at sundry times and different places participated, furnished subjects for interesting reminiscences. But it is not at all likely that Mr. Randall allowed to pass unimproved a good opportunity for speaking a word for his Master. The closing conversation warrants this assumption. General Stark, though professing to be a deist, was deeply affected, and with tearful eyes exclaimed: "God bless you! God bless you! God bless you! I am an old man and may stay here but a little while; but my wife is younger than I, and may outlive me. I shall charge her and my son ever to receive you and treat you with respect."

After an absence of about two weeks, Mr. Randall reached home, though nearly exhausted. He recorded: "There is not a

town between Ashby and New Durham
where I have not left traces of my blood in
very many places."

The August session of the Yearly Meeting was to occur at Adams, its new location.
Mr. Randall had purposed to attend. But
now that seemed impossible. As a substitute for his presence, he put some of his
struggling thoughts on paper and forwarded
them in the form of a letter:

NEW DURHAM, N. H., August 15, 1807.

Dear and well beloved in the Lord:

It is with a degree of trial and pleasure
that I salute you in this manner. Trial that
I cannot be with you in bodily presence, for
which I have been most anxiously longing;
and pleasure that this one resource is left
me, through which I, while absent in body,
can write, and thus bless you in the name of
the Lord.

Dear brethren, the cause of God is mine.
My soul's care and delight is to see it pros-
per. When able I have spared no labor,
either of body or mind, whether near or far,

Benjamin Randall

in heat or cold, by day or night, for the advancement of the same. And, glory to God! to this I have the testimony of a good conscience.

But my labors are almost ended, and I am about to receive my crown. My body is now too weak for me to go to Adams. But bless the Lord that I can be there in spirit and by letter! And I will take the liberty of giving a word of advice, as a father to his children, though with humility and respect.

First, to my dear brethren in the ministry: I feel much for you. Your lot is a particular one, and much, very much, depends upon you as to the promotion or destruction of the cause. You, in a certain sense, are like a city on a hill. All eyes are upon you. You profess to be the representatives of Jesus. Consider what an example he set for his ambassadors to follow. What humility! What meekness! What godliness! What holiness! Dear brethren, follow this advice, Walk in the example of Christ. And when the chief Shepherd shall appear, you shall receive a crown of glory that fadeth not away.

Benjamin Randall

Second, a word to all: Though enfeebled in body, my care for the cause remains undiminished. My mind travels to every part. And when looking back to 1780, the year when this denomination commenced, how thankful I feel for what God has done for us. My soul cries out with astonishment! " Oh, magnify the Lord with me, and let us exalt his name together! "

Brethren, we have become a somewhat numerous people, and I fear are not so humble as we should be. Let us, I pray, strive to be most Christlike. And, withal, let us keep the unity of the spirit in the bonds of peace. Let us cleave to the Scriptures— make them our only rule of faith and practice, both in temporal life and in church government.

But I have more things to utter than I can now write with pen and ink, and therefore must forbear.

Your servant for Christ's sake,

BENJAMIN RANDALL.

This letter, though expressed in the style and under conditions of a past century, is worthy of careful perusal and the most can-

[203]

Benjamin Randall

did consideration. It is good for all time and for all classes of Christians.

Somewhat revived, Mr. Randall was carried in his chaise to the Yearly Meeting held at Edgecomb, Maine. He was five days on the road, thus reaching his destination by easy stages.

The opening of the meeting was a touching scene. There was but the ghostly form of the once vigorous leader. All felt assured that he could be with them no more after this. It might seem like presumption, but the brethren were anxious for him to preach once more at their annual session, and to their pressing solicitations he yielded.

Mr. Randall was cheered and comforted by reports of prosperity from nearly all sections of the country covered by this conference. After making a few visits in the vicinity, all that his strength would allow, he took his final leave of what he had been accustomed to call his " New Vineyard."

After return from Edgecomb it might seem that he would now certainly take a rest. But the day following his arrival at home, the Sabbath, found him at the sanctuary preaching both forenoon and afternoon. Thus he kept on, occasionally recording in his journal, " Too sick to be out." In his case that meant much.

We have on record the attendance of Mr. Randall upon one more Yearly Meeting in Maine before the close of this, the last full year of his ministry. The meeting opened at Gorham, November seventh. In response to urgent requests he presided.

Among many items of business considered and acted upon at this session it was voted to grant the request of Vermont for the February session of the Yearly Meeting. The carrying of this motion into effect established the Vermont Yearly Meeting, the first session of which was held at Bradford, February, 1808.

But to return to Gorham. In connection with worship on the Sabbath, " the power of the Lord was wonderful." Monday was a most solemn and interesting day. A few

Benjamin Randall

prayers and exhortations followed the opening, but who should be " mouth for God "? All minds were instinctively turned toward one—the observed of all. They must hear him once more if possible. But how could he speak in his extreme weakness? Sitting there in his easy chair, pale and haggard, how could any expect to hear words from him? But no minister present seemed willing to move, though Mr. Randall urged that some brother would. For a time silence reigned in the meeting, impressive silence, broken at last by a request from Mr. Randall to one near, " Please help me to my feet."

He announced as his text 1 Peter 1 : 22: " Seeing ye have purified your souls in obeying the truth through the Spirit unto unfeigned love of the brethren, see that ye love one another with a pure heart fervently." For the time and circumstances no words could have been more fitting. His first utterances were hoarse and hardly audible. But as he proceeded his nervous energies

Benjamin Randall

roused, his utterance became stronger and louder, till his words rolled out with much the force and resonance of former days. The power of God supplemented all his natural forces, enabling him for the time to rise above his infirmities. Indeed, he seemed all voice—voice right from the presence-chamber of God, bringing words of big import, with burning eloquence.

When through with his final testimony for that region, and just ready to fall from exhaustion, he was gently helped to his chair. The scene was indescribable. Mr. Randall recorded in his journal:

The mighty power and glory of God were very refreshing. The Lord enabled me to speak with great freedom.

With deep emotion he took his departure from Maine, leaving many " sorrowing most of all, that they should see his face no more."

In closing the year Mr Randall made this record:

Benjamin Randall

Here ends my journal for 1807. From being so much unwell, I have traveled only two thousand five hundred and ninety-three miles and attended only two hundred and three meetings, besides weddings and religious visits.

XXVIII

FROM GRACE TO GLORY
1808

FOR a long time it had been evident that the separation of Mr. Randall's soul from his feeble body could only be a matter of a few months at the longest. The most of his remaining days can be regarded as only the last flickerings of a candle in its socket.

Mr. Randall regarded it as a special dispensation of grace that he was able to preach on the first Sabbath of the year, which he did from John 4 : 24, 26, and 29. The reaction necessitated his keeping his room for a few days. But he recovered strength enough to visit Alton, where he was caught in a violent storm and his return was impeded by snow-drifts. The following transcript is made from his journal of January seventeenth:

P

Benjamin Randall

At the house of God in much feebleness, yet the Spirit raised me up to speak from Luke 17 : 32. A solemn scene. Returned home in great weakness.

At the February Monthly Meeting in New Durham, while the brethren were enjoying a good season at the church, Mr. Randall says:

In my home confinement I felt moved to make a new surrender of myself to the Lord. Had I a thousand such souls as mine, I could trust them all with the Lord Jesus.

On the last day of February, which was the Sabbath, he was a little better, though very weak. He recorded:

Was carried by sleigh to God's house and spoke awhile, but was so overcome that with difficulty I was gotten home.

The matter of his material support during these months of physical decline is worthy of more than passing notice. He was a good financial manager, and during his

Benjamin Randall

effective years, by close calculation and economy, from the products of his little farm, and the benevolence of the people whom he served, he had succeeded in comfortably supporting his family. And now that his ability as a breadwinner had failed, it is interesting to note how some of his favorite texts of Scripture had illustration. Among these was: " Trust in the Lord, and do good; so shalt thou dwell in the land, and verily thou shalt be fed." Also this, " Lo, I am with you alway, even unto the end of the world."

Without human prearrangement, people at Sandwich, New Hampton, Portsmouth, and other parts of the State, made up loads of provisions, consisting of everything needful for family consumption, which were delivered at the door of the Randall house, each arriving when its contents was most needed. One of these loads was collected and delivered by two enterprising women who lived many leagues to the northwest of New Durham.

Benjamin Randall

When possible, Mr. Randall would be up, studying the Scriptures, writing, visiting, or doing whatever might seem most likely to promote the greatest good. During this last year the burden of his heart, with that of Paul, was " the care of all the churches."

As the May Quarterly Meeting approached, though in feebleness and suffering, he prepared his final address to the brethren. It manifests his mental vigor and spiritual devotion, and his abiding interest in all that could make for the welfare of the churches. It is as interesting as it is long, so long that only selected portions can here be given. It is noteworthy that in this last written message he still holds to the simple name—to his heart so dear—BAPTIST.

NEW DURHAM, N. H., May 18, 1808.

To the Baptist Quarterly Meeting to hold at Andover, N. H.

My very dear Brethren and Friends:

I thank God that, as a disciple of Jesus, I am permitted once more to write you.

Benjamin Randall

May the God of grace manifest his presence and power in your assembly and roll the weight of his cause upon your souls. May your meeting together be more than simply to salute each other, rejoice together, pray, praise, preach, and go home happy. It may properly be all this, but it should be more, *much more!*

My dear brethren in the ministry, you are precious in the sight of the Lord, and exceedingly precious to my soul. I know your work is great. I know your trials are many—within and without. You greatly fear that you will not do your work aright and agreeable to the mind of God. You go to it with trembling in view of its greatness and your own weakness.

But be not discouraged. The Lord will stand by you and give you strength equal to your day. Only trust in him and he will be all you want or need in every state.

I must here set my seal to this point. I have been in the ministry of God's word thirty-one years last March, and have ever found him, in every state, all I needed. And bless his wonder-working name, he is that to me at the present moment! His grace is

Benjamin Randall

everything in sickness and in health. How wonderfully has that grace been displayed to me during my long, tedious confinement! It has made my prison a palace. I have never had one moment of discontent or impatience. Neither have I thought the time long. But I have had such overpowering manifestations of God's love that I could not contain them.

I am more and more confirmed in the doctrines which the Lord gave me to preach. I remain strong in the faith of our Lord Jesus Christ. I am sitting and waiting for whatever the will of my Father may be, and I know he will do all things right.

Ye ministers of Jesus, how happy is your lot! How glorious your reward! Not only *hereafter*, but *here!* Never utter a complaining word. Why, there is no other such a state attainable this side of glory! No state so heavenly as that of a minister of Jesus Christ! What a heaven of heavens it is! How is my soul enraptured when calling to mind the glorious scenes I have enjoyed in my ministry! This is reward enough for wearing out a thousand lives, were they as long as the longest that ever lived.

[214]

Benjamin Randall

Cheer up! Cheer up! Ye poor, yet rich; ye weak, yet strong; ye trembling, yet valiant ministers of Jesus. Wear out in the cause and rejoice in the privilege!

Saints, arise, shine! Hold on and hold out! I will soon meet you in glory. Pray for your unworthy brother. I die, your servant for Jesus' sake,

BENJAMIN RANDALL.

During the next five months Mr. Randall was not only confined to his house, but for the most part to his bed. He received many visitors, and religious services were occasionally held at his home, much to the edification of his soul, ready to receive as to impart some spiritual gift.

A few hours before his death the Lord gave him strength for a brief space, so that he talked, prayed, and praised God loud enough to be heard in an adjoining room. Then followed a relapse, from which he rallied only enough to whisper, " My soul is full of Jesus. I long to depart." Here his strength failed again, and we may fittingly

Benjamin Randall

allow Pope to express, in substance, what
he might have said:

> Vital spark of heavenly flame,
> Quit, oh, quit this mortal frame;
> Trembling, hoping, lingering, flying—
> Oh, the pain, the bliss of dying!
>
> The world recedes; it disappears;
> Heaven opens on my eyes; my ears
>   With sounds seraphic ring;
> Lend, lend your wings; I mount, I fly!
> O grave, where is thy victory?
>   O death, where is thy sting?

At two o'clock in the morning of October
22, 1808, the white soul of Benjamin Randall went out and up. This was on Monday,
and the funeral occurred four days later.
Rev. John Buzzell, the one chosen to conduct the services, says: " Mr. Randall settled all his temporal concerns, made every
arrangement in respect to his funeral, indicated the man to preach the sermon, and
planned the order of the procession."

The host present at the funeral was a
reminder of the most largely attended
Yearly Meetings at New Durham. Mr. Buz-

zell announced his text from 2 Timothy
4 : 7, 8: "I have fought a good fight, I
have finished my course, I have kept the
faith." Seventeen ordained ministers were
present. Six, the oldest, served as bearers.
One walked with the widow. The other ten
took their places next to the relatives, as
mourners. In the rear of these the local
church-members fell into line. Then followed Mr. Randall's physicians. Next, all
civil and military officers present. Finally,
citizens in general. These aggregated a very
long procession, forcibly reminding one of
the event described in Acts 8 : 2: "And
devout men carried Stephen to his burial
and made great lamentation over him."

Mr. Randall's wife survived him till May
12, 1826. They had eight children: Robert
Oram, Mary Shannon, Benjamin Walton,
Margaretta Frederica, Ursula, William,
Joanna, and Henry Allen.

There can be no more fitting closing of
this chapter than a transcript of a record
found in the " Free Baptist Cyclopedia ":

[217]

Benjamin Randall

September 14, 1859, the plain marble slab that marked the resting-place of Benjamin Randall was replaced by a beautiful monument of Italian marble, erected by the denomination. Over one thousand persons listened to the impressive religious services at the dedication.

He sleeps amid the beauties of nature. Pleasant fields are all around. The wind in the forest at the southeast chants a requiem; a rivulet southwest glides peacefully along, and all day long the sun rests graciously upon that hilltop.

Benjamin Randall

THE RANDALL MONUMENT

[219]

XXIX

MR. RANDALL IN PEN-PICTURE

HAVING followed Mr. Randall through his early life and public labors, we may now consider him in his person—in what he was as a man, and in some of the conditions of his success in the ministry.

In stature Mr. Randall was about five feet nine inches, of an erect, compact build—well formed in every way. His hands were small and delicate; chest, full; forehead, high and broad; eyes, dark gray, approaching hazel in color; nose, Grecian in form; mouth, expressive of firmness; hair, dark auburn, worn long as was the manner of the times—especially with clergymen. Mr. Randall threw his hair back in negligee, but it had a tendency to part in the middle and curl, which he deplored, as he thought it might be regarded by some as savoring of vanity on his part.

Benjamin Randall

His movements were energetic but graceful. His mind was quick to comprehend, of a meditative turn, inclined to look thoroughly into things. He was not given to credulity, believing only on conclusive evidence. His order, as the phrenologists would say, was prominent; taste, delicate; conscientiousness, large; will, when once convinced by evidence, unyielding. He was firm to dictates of duty and fearless of danger. In short, the prominent characteristics of Mr. Randall were such as combine in heroes and martyrs.

As to clothing, Mr. Randall selected good material, and would be satisfied with nothing short of a perfect fit. His coat was of clerical cut. Till late in life he wore trousers of the colonial style, buckled at the knee, with long hose and broad-buckled shoes.

Before failing health required an easier mode of travel, Mr. Randall rode on horseback. But during his last years, except in winter, when he used a sleigh, he rode in a chaise. This allowed his wife to accompany

Benjamin Randall

him, which was at times a necessity. When riding on horseback, he wore a kind of overalls to protect his clothing from dust and mud. At the end of his journey he removed this outer garment and then, with but little attention to his person, he appeared presentable.

Himself a model of neatness, he could hardly see how a real sloven could enter the kingdom of heaven. We are not to regard this carefulness about dress as the outcropping of vanity, but rather as arising from his natural love of order. That trait would have compelled him to the same course if, like Robinson Crusoe, he had been the sole occupant of an island.

Naturally kind-hearted, frank, and generous, Mr. Randall was inclined to make all about him happy. His influence was like that of the gentle dew—unobtrusive but refreshing. This nature, supplemented by the grace of God, gave him access to the hearts of all ages and all classes.

One element of personal power was the

fact that, like Savonarola, he knew his Bible and believed in his divine mission. Another element was his strong, unwavering faith in God. What was said of another great religious leader, with slight adaptation, is equally applicable to Mr. Randall:

He was a man of audacious courage because of absolute faith. He believed that Christianity was adapted to the universal needs of humanity. He believed that humanity had a capacity, God-given, to apprehend and accept Christianity. His courage carried with it a great hope. He believed, really believed, that one with God was a majority; and he constantly acted on that belief. With all this intensity of spiritual conviction, and consequent courageous hopefulness, he resembled neither the mystics nor the monks. He belonged neither to the Pietists nor the Puritans. He was intense without being narrow, bold without being pugnacious, and spiritual without being ascetic.

If Mr. Randall had been a college graduate the fact would have been much more

Benjamin Randall

gratifying to a not altogether unjustifiable pride on the part of his disciples. As it was, he had fair school privileges, considering the times, and he improved them. He collected all available literature and was an omnivorous reader. What Dr. Newell Dwight Hillis said of Horace Greeley has equal application to Mr. Randall:

God gave him a hungry mind, which literally consumed facts of nature and life. Like a locust, he consumed every dry twig and every green branch of knowledge. He was trained in the school of experience, and graduated at the university of hard knocks.

In addition to a large stock of general information, Mr. Randall was mighty in the Scriptures; and his logical turn of mind gave his message homiletical order. But the most important factor of his furnishings was the enduement of the Holy Spirit. Without this he felt himself utterly unfit for sacred service. But "after that the Holy Ghost had come" upon him, he could say with Isaiah: "The Lord God hath given me the tongue of the learned, that I should know how to speak a word in season."

Mr. Randall systematized the religious doctrines of the Bible as he understood them, and sustained each with the strongest proof-texts bearing upon it. He did not wrench any of these doctrines out of their proper relations to others, but held and taught them as a harmonious whole.

As a matter of fact, it may be said that, as to essentials, Mr. Randall projected that system of doctrines a hundred years beyond his times, and the churches are now busy pushing them over the world.

XXX

THE MINISTRY UNDER RANDALL

A S churches began to multiply under the ministry of Mr. Randall and his associate laborers, the questions of church government and church nurture were forced upon their consideration. It was seen that this work naturally divided itself into departments, and was likely to be more efficiently done if committed to different classes of ministers. It was found that such an arrangement would be entirely compatible with the parity of the ministry and with New Testament usages. Hence there arose the orders in the ministry known as teaching elders, ruling elders, licentiates, and lay preachers.

In Randall's times the highest order of ministers in the denomination were called teaching elders. The prefix was to indicate, in part, the nature of their work, and in part to differentiate them from ruling elders. They were expected to be as thoroughly informed as possible as to the doctrines and usages held by the denomination, and to transmit a knowledge of the same to the developing ministry, who in turn should "be able to teach others also." They were to administer the ordinances and, under direction of conference, though local in residence, serve the churches at large as evangelists. Above all, they were to preach the Lord's gospel in its fulness.

The nurture of the churches required pastoral attentions which the teaching elders, because of the itinerant nature of their work, could not give. Hence the order of ruling elders. The ruling elder was a local pastor. He was to act as standing moderator in all meetings of the church, inspect the state of the treasury, approve the records, and, with the clerk, sign all church documents. He was to "improve his gift publicly, as God might call, and administer the ordinances in case of the sickness or absence of a teaching elder." This order, with its necessity, passed with the settlement of teaching elders as pastors. Then also the prefix "teaching" dropped out of use, and ordained ministers were known simply as elders.

Licentiates were licensed preachers in training for ordination. They might perform all the functions of the regular ministry, except the administration of the ordinances.

Lay preachers might appoint and conduct religious services as opportunity should open, and as they might interpret the will of God. Members of this order were useful as general assistants in church work, and some who began as lay preachers developed into teaching elders.

For assignment, ministers of all grades held themselves subject to the direction of Quarterly or Yearly Meetings. It was the custom of churches, and even of communities where there was no religious organization, to apply to the sessions for minis-

Benjamin Randall

terial help. These requests would be considered in connection with available forces in the ministry, and assignments made accordingly.

When a brother thus received an appointment, he was considered in duty bound to go, whether he had been previously consulted in the matter or not. And entire submission was the rule. These missions might terminate in a few days, or continue for several weeks, as the interest might indicate.

Respecting material support, for the first forty years of its organic life, about the only reward the denomination could offer its ministry was that of Mazzini, the Italian patriot, to the young men of his country, *"Come and suffer."* A paragraph in Doctor Stewart's history on this subject deserves the transcription which, in substance, is here given it.

: It was then an untried experiment to leave the support of the ministry to the voluntary contributions of the people. But it was the gospel ground, and Free Baptist

Benjamin Randall

ministers were ready to hazard their all in
the trial. So anxious were they to secure
their end—the removal of all coercive means
for sustaining the cause of Christ—that
they voluntarily subjected themselves to
great privations and hardships.

They not only refused to be supported by
taxes imposed by law, but generally declined
to be parties to an agreement for stipulated
salaries, receiving only what individuals
were disposed to give. And during this
transition state, this breaking down of a
long-established compulsory usage, and the
building up of a voluntary one, during a
period of nearly forty years, the Free Baptist ministry stood as a pledge to the world
that religion would be sustained and the
spiritual wants of the people would be cared
for, without the aid of civil law.

Such a revolution in the church could not
be effected without sacrifice. And God
raised up those self-denying men to show
what could and would be done by a Church
cut loose from State patronage. God gave

Benjamin Randall

freely of his spirit to our fathers, and they laid all upon the altar of consecration. They would be satisfied only when men were left as free to sustain religion as they were to accept it. And they succeeded. But our people saw later that it was entirely consistent with the voluntary support of the ministry that pledges be made in advance and paid as needed, on the instalment plan.

As to education, the preliminary training of ministers under Randall was much the same as that of doctors, lawyers, and civic officers of the times. They had generally the best furnishings that the common schools could give them, and picked up additional equipment on their respective lines as opportunity opened.

The young men of our people who felt called to the ministry pushed specific preparatory studies by the use of the best helps available. Respecting books, whatever they had or lacked, the Bible was their principal text-book. Perhaps the very paucity of general literature enabled them the better to

[231]

Benjamin Randall

concentrate their minds on this "compendium of all knowledge," as a great author has called the Bible.

An eminent literary authority has said: "If you want to make a versatile man, turn a boy loose in a library. If you want a boy to have distinction, lock him out of a library, and send him into solitude with the English Bible, Bunyan's 'Pilgrim's Progress,' and Æsop's 'Fables.'" Mr. Lincoln was a pretty good illustration of this statement; for, after his six months in a log schoolhouse, these three books constituted his library during his formative years. In speaking of the Bible, Scott called it the incomparable book. Froude said that the Bible was in itself a liberal education.

From a large accumulation of facts, showing that our fathers made the study of the Scriptures a specialty, a few are subjoined. Rev. Ebenezer Knowlton, the son of a minister associated with Randall, says: "My father, Elders Perkins, Clark, Place, Dyer, and others used to sit hours together in our

Benjamin Randall

front room, with Bible and concordance in hand, studying and proving to each other what the Scriptures teach." Thus, in their private studies, parlor gatherings, and ministers' conferences, like the noble Bereans, "they received the word with all readiness of mind, and searched the Scriptures." The thoroughness of this search, and the familiarity attained with the Scriptures, was, in many cases, remarkable. Occasionally one became almost a living concordance; while most of them were able readily to turn to any passage desired without consulting a concordance.

But, however important a knowledge of the Scriptures may be, for greatest efficiency ministers need more. Special schools for the training of our ministry had establishment later, but none of these existed during the first decades of our denominational history.

As the best available substitute for something better, in 1793 elders' conferences were organized. These developed into veri-

Benjamin Randall

table divinity institutes. They were held in different places covered by the churches. The sessions were held four times a year, and sometimes continued several days. The constituency included teaching elders, ruling elders, licensed preachers, lay preachers, and deacons. Of these, there were sometimes more than fifty in attendance.

Among the benefits sought by these institutes were harmony in doctrine, sermonic methods, pulpit decorum, and pastoral efficiency. The substance of the oral instructions given appeared later in works on doctrinal theology, homiletics, sacred rhetoric, pastoral theology, and other subjects taught in divinity schools.

Respecting results of these sessions, the following paragraph, taken from Stewart's " History," may be accepted as good authority:

The influence of these meetings was highly beneficial; occurring as they did, four times a year, and continuing as they did, for two days, including much of the intervening

Benjamin Randall

night. The lectures of those wise, experienced, and, some of them, learned men, must have been interesting, instructive, and useful. The elders' conference was, indeed, a most excellent and instructive school.

Hosea Quinby, D. D., a college graduate, and for many years principal of high-grade schools, in referring to these conferences, speaks in stronger terms than does Doctor Stewart respecting their beneficial effects upon our early ministry.

With a knowledge of facts which warranted the assertions of these two conservative men, we are forced to admit that our fathers, in these conferences and other assemblies, and by private study secured to themselves the very best means available for developing their minds and otherwise preparing themselves for the work committed to their charge.

As to their success, the following incidents are illustrative. An aged lawyer of Boston, a Congregationalist, said in substance:

Benjamin Randall

In my younger days I was accustomed, more or less frequently, to listen to some of the men Randall trained. When fully aroused to their subject they were men of real power, mighty in the Scriptures. I often hear those from Andover, but none are equal in the word of God to these men.

Another incident is to the point. A minister trained after the manner of Randall preached one half day in Portland, Maine, and a college-educated minister preached in the same pulpit the other half. A number of lawyers, being in the city at the time, heard both. After the last service, as they were together, one who was acquainted with the preachers remarked: "One of the men who preached to-day had college education and the other had not; which was the college man?" The unanimous answer indicated the one who had been trained under Randall as the college man.

Because the fathers were human, they had faults and limitations. But, as a rule, they were men of sterling sense, deep piety, and high purpose. They adapted themselves to the times in which they lived. God gave them a work, and they did it. He gave them a message, and they delivered it. God accepted their efforts, and abundantly blessed them for the betterment of both Church and State.

When the fathers are mentioned it behooves us, their spiritual descendants, to lift our hats and bow very low.

But new times demand new men and improved methods. With the lapse of time, competition in all departments of business has grown sharper, and demands upon all learned professions have become more exacting.

Here behold the providence of God! Just in proportion to the advancement of standards has been the increase in educational facilities.

Divinely called young men are needed for the service of the churches. But those who would emulate the fathers must adjust themselves to the exigencies of current

Benjamin Randall

times. To do their best work for humanity
and for God, they must avail themselves of
the best culture possible to them. They must
then have all their natural and acquired
abilities supplemented by POWER FROM ON
HIGH.

PART II

POSTHUMOUS INFLUENCE

XXXI

THE LARGER GROWTH OF A FOUNDER'S THOUGHTS

IT has been said that the distinguishing features of any religious body, however remote from its origin, may be traced to the characteristics of its founder; that, however diversified its operations, these operations are but expansions of germs present in the heart, if not ideals, of its founder.

Whoever has carefully studied the subject of the preceding chapters must recognize the application of this general statement to the relations of the Free Baptist denomination to Benjamin Randall.

Are we insistent upon a regenerated membership? Mr. Randall would accept none except on the clearest evidence of such an experience.

Have we an efficient system of church government? The system which he be-

Benjamin Randall

queathed to the denomination, with a few modifications and expansions to adapt it to new conditions, is still operative and ideal.

Have we our several departments of missions? Mr. Randall spent his effective life in home mission work, and the Master's last commission was a favorite theme of his preaching.

Have we a popular sentiment for education and for educational institutions of all grades? Mr. Randall was respectably educated for his times, was a lifelong student, and advocated the largest possible education of his disciples.

Have we, as a people, always been in the forefront of temperance reform? Mr. Randall was a total abstainer, and smote with giant blows the drinking customs of his times.

Were our people pioneers in the antagonism to American slavery? Benjamin, when a boy, accompanied his father, Captain Randall, to Southern ports, and while the ship's cargo was being handled, witnessed the

Benjamin Randall

crack of the driver's whip which drew blood from the bare backs of slaves. His tender heart was shocked by the sight; and during his ministry he both privately and publicly declared against the system of slavery.

Are we giving special attention to the religious education of our children and young people? Mr. Randall held special meetings for the religious instruction of children and youth; and wherever he went these classes flocked around him for the pleasant greetings with which he always saluted them.

We are quite sure that those best acquainted with the spirit which animated the subject of this story will sustain the assertion that our efforts for a regenerated membership, an expanded church, a world-wide evangelism, an educated constituency, and all-round reforms are emanations from the heart of Benjamin Randall.

It is fitting that some of these posthumous influences which have taken organized form, as well as others which refuse classification, have more specific mention.

XXXII

CHURCH GOVERNMENT

OUR system of church government is democratic in that it arises from its constituency. It is modeled after American civil government. The local church represents the town; the Quarterly Meeting or Association, the county; the Yearly Meeting, the State; and General Conference, the nation.

For thirty-five years after the organization, in 1792, of the first Yearly Meeting, that was the highest tribunal of the denomination. But, as the circle of churches enlarged, and Yearly Meetings increased, the greatest efficiency demanded a central organization that could develop and direct philanthropic enterprises and properly represent the denomination to the world. On October 11-14, 1827, that body became the General Conference.

REV. ENOCH PLACE
Moderator of the First General Conference

Benjamin Randall

This first conference convened at Tunbridge, Vermont. In addition to its delegates it had a large attendance, in which several States were represented. The business sessions were held mornings and evenings, leaving the afternoons for meetings of worship. Reports were received from the several Yearly Meetings, which included revivals, accessions to churches, new churches organized, church edifices built, ministers ordained, and so forth. All business introduced was referred to appropriate committees, and action upon their reports constituted the principal business of the conference.

As matters that had consideration, and upon which opinions were recorded at the conference, show the mental and spiritual trend of the fathers, a few are here noted.

It was agreed that regeneration and baptism were essential to church-membership; that each church should have full authority to discipline its own members, but a minister should not be received or excluded

Benjamin Randall

without the advice of an elders' conference or a council of ministers; that church, Quarterly Meeting, and Yearly Meeting clerks make their annual reports with great care, giving full statistics; that the ministry must be experimentally pious, called of God, led by the Spirit, and holy in life.

Doctor Stewart, in referring to the men who constituted this first conference, says: "Their wisdom is seen in the fact that they attempted but little, yet accomplished much."

The conference had a cordial reception by the local church and community, and generous entertainment was provided. The delegates parted in love, having an increased attachment each for the other, and returned to their respective fields with broadened views and increased love for humanity and for God.

In order to get the business of the denomination thoroughly in hand, the conference held its next six sessions annually, and the four succeeding, biennially. Since then they have been held triennially.

Benjamin Randall

At the session of the conference held in 1871, arrangements were made for the appointment of a Conference Board. This Board became a fact at the next session, held in 1874. At first it consisted of seven members, but in the 1892 session they were increased to twenty-one, one-third of whom should be women.

The duties imposed upon this Board were many and various, but may be included in this provision: It was to " Act for the conference in the interim of sessions."

In 1894 the missionary societies, education society, and other benevolent organizations of the denomination were placed under the executive management of the Conference Board.

Judged by the standard of best results for the least expenditure of time, labor, and treasure, our system of government, from church to General Conference, is nearly or quite ideal.

XXXIII

ATTITUDE AS TO INTOXICANTS

IN the early years of our national history liquors were used as a panacea, and most of the well used them as preventives. Mr. Randall was subject to attacks of acute colic. When thus taken on the road he would sometimes call at the nearest house for relief. The remedy generally offered, and as often declined, was liquor. Mr. Randall was a total abstainer, and never lost a good opportunity to antagonize the drinking customs of his times. His disciples were like-minded, and their public utterances against the use of intoxicants were so far in advance of their times as to be seldom well received, and often brought upon them mob violence.

As early as 1820, Rev. John Buzzell, of Maine, because of his activity in temperance reform, had become very unpopular with

Benjamin Randall

rumsellers and certain lewd fellows of the baser sort. Threats of personal violence were in the air, and some of them came to his ears. But if they had any effect, they deepened his purpose to throw the full weight of his influence against an evil so intrinsically and manifestly wicked.

A desperado chose his opportunity on Portland bridge, over which he knew Mr. Buzzell must pass on a certain night, in order to reach his home at Parsonsfield. As Mr. Buzzell approached the center of the bridge he was confronted by one whom he knew to be a local tough. After declaring his murderous purpose and emphasizing it with a blood-curdling oath, the fellow drew a pistol, took deliberate aim, and fired. At that instant Mr. Buzzell's horse stumbled and fell upon one knee, allowing the bullet to pass harmlessly over his master's head. Buzzell, in that deep, mellow voice which made the gospel message that fell from his lips so effective, calmly replied, "Vengeance is mine; I will repay, saith the Lord." The

Benjamin Randall

authorities, by the interposition of Mr. Buzzell, were dissuaded from making an arrest. But death, in the form of retributive justice, as it would seem, fell upon the man; and just one week from the time of the encounter on the bridge, Mr. Buzzell was called to conduct his funeral.

The first general temperance awakening began in 1826, with the organization, in Boston, of the American Temperance Society. Free Baptists, who for several years, and in different parts of the country, had been engaged in the work that this body was organized to do, at once became its coadjutors.

Twenty-five years later Gen. Neal Dow was leading a temperance campaign over Maine, which culminated in the first State prohibitory law. That movement had no more fearless champions than Free Baptist ministers; it had no more loyal supporters at the polls than Free Baptist laymen.

Free Baptist women have not only favored the temperance crusade led by their breth-

ren, but have been in it. While the work of
the great majority has been of a quiet and
educational nature, many have distinguished
themselves in associated efforts, through the
press and from the platform.

For instance, Mrs. E. Burlingame Cheney,
wife of Doctor Cheney, late president of
Bates College, former editor of " The Missionary Helper," now a member of the General Conference Board, as president of the
Rhode Island Woman's Christian Temperance Union, was a potent factor in securing
State constitutional prohibition for 1884-
1887. To accomplish this, she planned,
worked, wrote, and lectured to the end of
the campaign. As a prominent lawyer was
passing from a crowded opera-house at the
close of one of her lectures, he remarked:
" I never heard that subject so ably handled
before." A leading politician of another
city, referring to this effort, said, " I never
saw a presidential campaign better managed."

The first woman to be honored by a niche

Benjamin Randall

in our National Hall of Fame—whose statue was, with fitting ceremonies, unveiled on February 17, 1905—was Frances E. Willard. One of her biographers said that she was descended from a noble, religious ancestry. Just so. Miss Willard's parents, her grandparents on both sides, and her great-grandmother on her father's side, were Free Baptists. As many letters by her own hand clearly testify, Miss Willard loved her ancestral church, and united with another only as a matter of local convenience. And such were the moral and spiritual conditions under which she was evolved who was declared to be, at the unveiling of her statue, "THE WORLD'S GREATEST WOMAN TEMPERANCE WORKER."

The first session of General Conference did but little more than organize. At the second session, held in 1828, among the principles for which it declared was that of temperance reform. If all its utterances on the subject, from that time to the close of the last session, were compiled, they would make

Benjamin Randall

a respectable volume. These declarations evince intelligent adaptation to their respective times and the current conflicts. They all had able discussion on the floor of conference, and were duly given to the public in periodical literature.

General Conference is a fair exponent of the denomination for which it stands. The leading political parties—and some of the lesser ones—are always represented in its constituency; yet its action has always been non-partisan. It believes in and advocates abstinence for the individual and prohibition for the nation; but courteously concedes the right of individual conscience respecting the political party through which each may seek local or national righteousness. Among recent utterances of conference on temperance reform were these words:

" WE WILL NEVER RETREAT, WE WILL NEVER CHANGE OUR POSITION EXCEPT TO ADVANCE, AND WE WILL BE HEARD."

[253]

XXXIV

HOME MISSIONS

IN the early settlement of New England many isolated communities were without the common means of grace. Mr. Randall and his colaborers felt themselves especially commissioned to carry the gospel to such communities. Like Paul, they were "ambitious to preach the gospel, not where Christ was already named, lest" they "should build upon another man's foundation," but in localities neglected and to people for whom no religious privileges had been provided.

At first these missionaries went forth on their own initiative, moved by their own interpretation of God's will. Sometimes their motives were misunderstood, and they met with opposition—even persecution. But generally they were cordially welcomed, and revivals followed their efforts.

REV. JOHN COLBY
A Pioneer Home Missionary

Benjamin Randall

After the establishment of Quarterly and Yearly Meetings, representatives of such destitute localities would in some cases send petitions to these assemblies for religious help. Such requests were always laid before the conference and considered with favor, and assignments were made according to evangelists available. An ideal team for evangelism would consist of two—an ordained minister and a licensed preacher as his assistant. In travel, the " elder " would commonly be on horseback and his disciple trudging at his side.

Soon after the passing of Mr. Randall, his successors in the ministry seemed simultaneously inspired with the spirit of church extension. Voluntary missionaries, trusting in God and the people for support, not only vigorously sustained the work in New England, but enlarged their circle of evangelistic work. Conspicuous among these missionaries was John Colby, who, at the age of twenty-two, left his home in Sutton, Vermont, for a horseback journey to Ohio and

Benjamin Randall

Indiana. In his outward journey he passed through southern New York and Pennsylvania. After visiting various parts of the States mentioned, he returned by way of Lake Erie and Niagara Falls. He suffered great hardships, was absent from home eight months, preached at nearly every halting-place, and traveled more than three thousand miles. Later, a string of churches sprang up the full length of his trail—traceable to his evangelistic efforts.

After the organization of the Home Mission Society, in 1834, evangelistic work and church-building were systematically pushed over the Middle States to the extreme Western frontier. The funds of this Society have paid church debts, built church edifices, and in part, or fully, sustained pastors at strategic points. Some of our largest and most useful churches have become such because of timely grants from the treasury of the Home Mission Society.

XXXV

FOREIGN MISSIONS

WHILE pagan nations were shut in by walls of granite or superstitions more impregnable, God allowed the churches of our country to increase their numbers and develop their resources. But with the providential opening of iron doors, special emphasis was placed upon the Lord's last commission, and the churches were moved to undertake world-wide evangelization. The eyes of our people were opened in the great awakening, and they became a factor of the general effort.

Such a succession of providences combined in associating our people with foreign missions as to justify a few words of explanation. The facts for this purpose have been gleaned from several of our publications, but mostly from the writings of Mrs. Hills, who, as far as they occurred in this

S   [257]

country, witnessed the scenes she graphically describes.

Amos Sutton, D. D., was an English General Baptist missionary in India. His wife was an American lady, the widow of Rev. Mr. Coleman, a Baptist missionary who joined Doctor Judson in Burma. Some time in 1830, Doctor Sutton, while contemplating the dense multitudes of heathen about him, and the fewness of his associate laborers, became heartsick and despondent. In an effort to encourage him, she suggested that he make an effort to induce the Free Baptists of America to join in their foreign mission work, as they were the same in doctrinal views as the General Baptists.

Doctor Sutton at once wrote a long letter, explaining the opportunity, and closing with these words: " Come, then, my American brethren; come over and help us. The way is as short and safe from India to heaven as from your land of privilege." After many months of delay, this letter reached its destination and was published in " The

Benjamin Randall

Morning Star," of April 13, 1832. This, with other articles on the same line, led to the organization, in 1833, of our Foreign Mission Society.

A little later Doctor Sutton visited this country for the recuperation of his health and the enlistment of recruits for the field. While here he traveled extensively and lectured often.

September 22, 1835, Doctor Sutton, his wife, and nineteen recruits stood on Union Wharf, Boston, ready to embark on the ship Louvre for India. Of these, Jeremiah Phillips and Eli Noyes, with their wives, were Free Baptists. Now let Mrs. Hills, then the wife of Rev. David Marks, describe the send-off:

Mr. Marks and myself being in Boston for the purpose of completing arrangements for the voyage of the missionaries, it was our precious privilege to be present in the throng of several thousand assembled on the wharf to witness the departure of the Louvre. The missionaries stood together

[259]

Benjamin Randall

on the side of the ship facing the throng, with cheerful faces, undimmed by a single tear. There were singing and prayer on the wharf, after which Mr. Sutton, as he looked upon the various groups of weeping friends on the shore, said: " This is not a sorrowful day to us. It is the happiest day I ever saw. We are going to preach the gospel to the heathen. Do you, in this Christian land, be careful that you do not neglect us. If you do, how will those condemn you to whom we are going! Think of that."

At eleven o'clock in the forenoon, the red-shirted seamen came on deck, up went the sails, the cable was cast off, and as the vessel moved slowly from its moorings the missionaries commenced to sing:

> " Yes, my native land, I love thee;
> All thy scenes, I love them well,"

and continued till their voices were lost in the distance. We gazed till the ships appeared a mere speck, and vanished from our sight.

Limited space must exclude details of the long voyage, the establishing of our mission,

Benjamin Randall

the hardships endured, the graves that soon closed over loved ones, and of victories finally gained. Here it must suffice to say that, of the large company of missionaries who sailed on the Louvre, Rev. Jeremiah Phillips, our senior missionary, was the last to leave the field.

Reenforcements soon followed our pioneers, stations were slowly increased, and in successive order came schools, churches, orphanages, homes for widows, medical dispensaries, and the printing-press.

Our Board, as a rule, has been fortunate in the selection of men and women for the field; the missionaries have faithfully served and honored the denomination that sustained them.

XXXVI

EDUCATIONAL WORK

DURING the generation immediately following the passing of Mr. Randall our ministers did a grand work in evangelization. Our numerical strength increased by leaps and bounds. Our denominational standards had invaded two British Provinces and were rapidly moving westward.

But the thoughtful among our ministry clearly saw that the greater efficiency of our denomination demanded that more be done by way of the general education of our young people and the special education of candidates for the ministry.

In the autumn of 1839 this sentiment began to take practical form. Four ministers—John Chaney, Silas Curtis, Dexter Waterman, and John J. Butler—met at Farmington, Maine, and after prayerful deliberation determined to call an educational

PROF. J.J. BUTLER, D.D.

REV. D. WATERMAN

REV. JOHN FULLONTON, D.D.

REV. JOHN CHANEY

REV. SILAS CURTIS

EDUCATIONAL PIONEERS

Doctors Butler and Waterman, Chaney and Curtis were
founders of the Free Baptist Education Society;
Doctor Fullonton was early and for many years
President of its first Divinity School

Benjamin Randall

convention. That call was then and there formulated. Later, with forty-six signatures, it was published in " The Morning Star." In response to this call on the fifteenth of January, 1840, seventy-six ministers and prominent laymen met at Acton, Maine, and organized the Free Baptist Education Society.

In ways that cannot here be mentioned, and to an extent incalculable, the Education Society has benefited our denomination and the world. In 1894 its work, with that of other benevolent societies, was placed under the executive management of the General Conference Board.

The primary object of the Society was the education of young men for the ministry. It has done this and much more. The sentiment that here had organic expression, through our periodical literature and pulpits, soon became general, and educational institutions sprang up over the denomination almost as by magic.

The educational sentiment of our people,

Benjamin Randall

and the expression of it, includes what has been called "the last word in popular education." McClure, in a recent magazine article, refers to the Chautauqua movement as "the last word in popular education." He then speaks of its systematic study of the Bible, its courses in arts, crafts, and domestic science; its programs of lectures, music, and different phases of entertainment. Our Ocean Park combines all that goes to make that last word in popular education, and more. With its deep pine grove and its broad sea-front, Ocean Park has local attractions that are impossible to Chautauqua on the lake.

At our denominational centennial, Doctor Bowen voiced the sentiment of our people as to the character of the schools we all want:

Our schools and colleges must be places where godliness shall be enthroned and promoted; where hope, light, and strength may go out to the church and the world. We are not wise in supporting them as simply literary institutions. We must labor and pray

Benjamin Randall

that their graduates may be positive Christian forces in the world. Our hope and success for the century upon which we have just entered depend upon the manner and spirit with which we solve this question of education. We must insist upon such an education as shall make citizens of usefulness and piety; uniting culture of intellect with spiritual growth and power. We want, America wants, the world wants, only consecrated men and women, who shall relieve its woes and bring peace and cheer.

Without fear of contradiction by any who know the facts, it is claimed that our schools have measured up to these high ideals. Rev. Granville C. Waterman, A. M., son of a founder of the Education Society, for several years recording secretary of that organization, and who had been principal of one of our seminaries, in referring to another institution of similar grade, said in part:

It is a *school*. That preeminently. It has never failed to give *instruction* to its students; to stimulate them to high resolve

Benjamin Randall

and resolute endeavor; to inspire in them a broad idea of true scholarship. This is fully proved by the rank they have taken in college and professional schools, and in the quality of the work they have done and are doing in the broader arena of the world's busy life.

It is a *Christian* school. From first to last there has always been within it a strong religious, but not sectarian, influence. Scores of young people, while in school there, have been led to begin a Christian life, and from a beginning there made have gone on from one degree of Christian attainment to another, until they have become pillars of strength to the churches in many parts of the country.

What Mr. Waterman wrote of the school that at that time filled his mind's eye is applicable to all our schools of similar and higher grades. Students from our seminaries and colleges have honored all positions in Church, State, and nation, from the lowest to the highest.

XXXVII

REMEMBERING THOSE IN BONDS AS BOUND WITH THEM

DURING the early part of the nineteenth century the influence of slavery, like the pall of death, hung over our country and cast its black shadow upon the whole nation. Civil government, the press, and even the pulpit were silent respecting this institution, or were its advocates. Doctor Cheney, late president of Bates College, in referring to these conditions, says:

The time, then, had come for Christian people to speak, else the nation, in the order of God's providence, might expect an early doom. And a Christian people did speak at the needed time, God—as I believe—making the choice. But the people God chose to speak for himself, to show the nation its sin, was not one strong in either numbers or wealth. This is not God's way of doing

Benjamin Randall

things. In the moral government of the world he means that no flesh shall glory in his presence. What people, then, did God choose to do this work? I answer, the Free Baptist people.

All students of history in possession of the facts must concede that these claims of Doctor Cheney are fully sustained. Our denomination was evolved during the revolutions that gave individuality to our nation. Among the characteristics of its natal inheritance, are a strong love of liberty, a keen sense of justice, and executive energy along all lines that make for purity of faith and righteousness of action.

Long before public expression on the subject, our people were in sympathy with the oppressed race of our nation. In 1834, in accordance with previous notice, a resolution in the interests of emancipation was passed by the Farmington, Maine, Quarterly Meeting. A few months later a similar resolution was adopted by the Rockingham, New Hampshire, Quarterly Meeting. The

Benjamin Randall

session of New Hampshire Yearly Meeting, in 1835, was held at Lisbon, with an estimated attendance of three thousand. In that great meeting, full of missionary interest and revival grace, the poor slave was not forgotten. Holding a paper in his hand, Rev. David Marks arose and said:

Brother Moderator: It is entirely proper for this Yearly Meeting to speak in behalf of the Africans. The church in America is guilty of the sin of slaveholding, because it has never come up and borne a firm and united testimony against it. Men tell us to be still, and wait for a more favorable opportunity. No, brethren, we must not be still; we must wash our hands from the guilt of this sin.

He then read and moved the adoption of the following:

Resolved, That the principles of immediate abolition are derived from the unerring word of God; and that no political circumstances whatever can exonerate Christians from exerting all their moral

Benjamin Randall

influence for the suppression of this heinous sin.

Rev. Jonathan Woodman, after enthusiastic remarks of approval, seconded the motion. After eloquent indorsement by others, including Amos Sutton, D. D., an English missionary from India, and F. A. Cox, D. D., of London, the motion was unanimously adopted.

Similar resolutions were soon adopted by our people in Vermont, New York, and Rhode Island. The General Conference was held the following October in Byron, New York. All constituent bodies were, by delegation, fully represented. At that session, conference unanimously adopted the following:

Resolved, That slavery is an unjust infringement on the rights of the slaves; an unwarrantable exercise of power on the part of the master; a potent enemy to the happiness and morals of our slaveholding population; and, if continued, must ultimately result in the ruin of our country.

Benjamin Randall

In 1839 General Conference declined an accession of twenty thousand members from Kentucky of similar faith and practice— except in the matter of slavery. This test act of Conference shut the door against the prospective reception of five thousand from North Carolina, and indefinite numbers of like faith from other Southern States. Doctor Stewart, in referring to this action, says:

It was a bold and unprecedented act for a denomination, in that day, thus to cast itself off from all connection with slavery. But the men who acted were the stuff of which heroes are made. And it is our joy that neither hope nor fear, flattery nor public scorn, could divert them from their convictions of right and duty.

Another item in this record concerns the position early taken by " The Morning Star," our denominational paper, on the question of slavery. For a long time the " Star " was the only religious journal in our country that met the question of slavery on high moral grounds.

Benjamin Randall

Our Anti-Slavery Society was organized in 1843, and from that time till slavery was abolished by constitutional amendment, the Society did valiant service by reports, addresses, and discussions, in keeping up a thrilling interest in emancipation.

As Christians our people had talked and prayed, and as citizens they had voted for emancipation. During 1861-1865 thousands of them, including fifty-eight of our ministers and more than two hundred of their sons, helped God answer their prayers, though " by terrible things in righteousness."

On the field of Gettysburg there stands a statue in bas-relief, placed there by a wealthy Philadelphian, who had heard the pathetic story which it represents. A Union soldier is shown bending over a wounded Confederate. With one arm the boy in blue supports the shoulders and head of the boy in gray, while with his other hand he gives him water from his canteen.

And this is the story: The Union regi-

ment was in double-quick charge. By a
change of orders it was for a moment, and
only a moment, at halt, when the faint call,
" Water! water! water! " caught the ear of
the Union boy. The rest of the story is told
in bas-relief. The hero of this episode was
and is a Free Baptist. For discretion and
bravery he was, soon after this act, ad-
vanced to a captaincy; he is now the Rev.
Ephraim W. Ricker, of New Hampshire.

The spirit that prompted the magnani-
mous act that stands memorialized in marble on the field of Gettysburg is the same
that animates our Free Baptist people. We
hold no grudge, rejoice with our Southern
fellow citizens over a free country, and
reach a fraternal hand to the entire commonwealth of Israel.

XXXVIII

WORK AMONG THE FREEDMEN

A S our denomination was the first to declare that "We will, as Christians and as Christian ministers, use our influence to promote the doctrine of emancipation," it was also among the first to act in response to General Butler's call for money and missionaries to evangelize and educate to citizenship the contrabands gathered at national strongholds in the South.

As soon as the Emancipation Proclamation had made it possible, this denomination was among the first to establish schools and churches for the freedmen. During the first six years of its opportunity, our Home Mission Board sent and sustained, in the interests of the freedmen, sixty-six different persons, pious and well educated, as teachers, and thirty-three ministers as missionaries.

Benjamin Randall

It took as fine courage for those pioneer teachers and missionaries to prosecute the work of education and evangelization as it did for the Union soldiers to make that work possible. It is fitting that those pioneer heroes and heroines be embalmed in the grateful memory of passing generations. Hence, with malice toward none, and love for all loyal citizens of our united country, a few of the conditions those pioneers had to reckon with, as gleaned from the copious scrap-book of Mrs. Anna S. Dudley Bates, are here given. The incidents, selected almost at random, are illustrative of others.

Under commission of the Free Baptist Home Mission Board, in company with three other ladies, Miss Dudley went to Virginia as a teacher of freedmen. She speaks of a cordial reception at Harper's Ferry by Rev. N. C. Brackett, who was local superintendent of Freedmen's Missions, and adds:

I had been at Harper's Ferry but a few days when it was proposed to open a school at Charlestown, eight miles up the Shenan-

Benjamin Randall

doah River. But it was not safe for a teacher to go alone, so General Van Patten, Chaplain Chase, Doctor Brackett, and a company of soldiers went as my escort; and I marched into Charlestown with bluecoats and bayonets leading the way.

The soldiers were left to guard the place for a while. But one morning I looked out and the soldiers were gone. For a moment my heart stood still with fear. Then, clear as human voice, came ringing through my soul: "The angel of the Lord encampeth round about them that fear him, and delivereth them," and my fear was gone.

I could get no permanent boarding-place for nearly two months. It would have been a lifelong disgrace for a Virginian to have boarded a Yankee teacher; and the Rubicon once passed, there could be no return to friends and society, no more than over the walls of caste in India. So I was there alone, boarding myself and teaching day and night, until I had a hundred and fifty pupils of all ages and complexions.

All the colored people manifested the greatest kindness toward us. I shall never forget the oft-repeated prayer: "O Lord,

Benjamin Randall

bless de teacher dat come so far distance to teach us. Front and fight her battles, and bring her safe home to glory—if you please, Massa Jesus."

But the white people of the locality made it clear that they had no use for Yankee schoolma'ms. Perhaps few of them could give as good a reason for their antipathy as did a local saloon-keeper, who, referring to Miss Dudley, said, " Every day Miss Massachusetts is in town I lose seventy dollars."

In writing of some of the dangers to which the teachers were exposed, Miss Dudley says:

Once I hardly dared to look at a weapon of war, but in the proud " Old Dominion " I have placed a good axe and six-shooter at the head of my bed many a night, resolved to sell my life as dearly as possible—if need be.

On one occasion, at least, this heroic courage was put to the test. Her living apartments were in the loft of her schoolroom.

Benjamin Randall

One morning the colored girl who stayed with her had to go early to service. Of course, in her departure she had left the door unbarred. Probably her movements had been watched, for soon Miss Dudley heard the approach of stealthy steps. She seized her axe and posed at the head of the stairs, where she was soon confronted by a lewd fellow of the baser sort. She raised the ax over his head and ordered a halt and retreat, immediate and unconditional. He looked at her just long enough to see that she meant business, then slunk down, out, and off.

But one more tragic incident can be admitted. Lexington was the center of Southern chivalry, and the location of the college over which General Lee presided and of one of our schools for the freedmen. The scrapbook relates the story:

These chivalrous (?) students had caused our teachers much trouble. One night a party of them gathered about the school building and demanded one of the scholars,

Benjamin Randall

saying they were going to shoot him. When
the teachers could not persuade them to go
away, and the rowdies were getting des-
perate, Miss Harper stepped forward and
told them if they shot Ben they would shoot
her first. With wonderful courage she
drove them away. The next day she had
them arrested and taken to court. The matter was hushed up, and General Lee sent the
teachers a note of apology. The next morning after this raid on the school, Ben was
sent to Lewiston, Maine.

To illustrate the spirit of sacrifice and desire for self-support on the part of those
who had just emerged from slavery, the
scrap-book gives us this:

We still feel encouraged in our work.
Instead of two hundred dollars, I have collected more than two thousand dollars for
churches here, and mostly from the colored
people in this place. They are all poor, and
the money given is earned by hard labor.
One cold, stormy day last winter, I found
an old woman, seventy years of age, trying
to wash. I was surprised, but she said, " O

Benjamin Randall

honey, I's tryin' to get a little mo' money for
de church." She had already given me five
dollars.

More than twenty years ago, Dr. Nathan
Cook Brackett, then president of Storer College, stated to the author:

But now, after almost three decades of
toil, the novelty of teaching bright-eyed
children and eager, grateful mothers their
first lessons from books has passed away.
So, also, to a large extent, has the heroism
of the work. One can now be a missionary
to the colored people and escape insult on the
street.

In response to a letter of inquiry respecting present Southern sentiment as to the
education of the colored race, after stating
that "in those sections where the educated
colored people are, there the sentiment in
favor of education is strongest," President
McDonald, of Storer College, then adds:

Here at Harper's Ferry we believe that
we are especially blest in the attitude of the

[280]

Benjamin Randall

best people in this matter. One hears nothing against the school from those whose opinion is worth considering. The same general attitude obtains in the whole village. We are thankful for that, and are trying to maintain so good a record that it will be impossible to have any other sentiment assert itself.

XXXIX

OUR WOMEN IN COOPERATIVE WORK

THE story of " Phaedrus; or, How We Got the Greatest Book in the World," by Newell Dwight Hillis, D. D., represents the celebration of Christmas Eve by a group of early disciples in the house of one Nicias, of Ephesus. The observance is very simple, consisting of what we might call a service of prayer, testimony, and praise. In it the very first speaker was a woman of rank, who was converted from heathenism, and who spoke as follows:

Whether or not the men of Greece follow the Master, all the women will. Too long we have had to work in silence, content to be neither seen nor heard when men were near. Because the Master was born of a woman on this night, it is become the night of nights for all the women of the world. He filled up the gulf between men and

women. When I learned that, I knew that
he would bring us the golden age.

The social gulf between men and women
was made by paganism, and wherever it
exists in nominally Christian lands, it is a
relic of paganism. " But from the beginning it was not so." Christ simply restored
women to the social relations that existed in
the Creative Mind.

As a people we have simply recognized
those relations. From the very first of our
organic existence, women have been conceded what we have regarded as their divinely appointed place, squarely by the side
of their brethren.

Our colleges were among the first to ignore sex discrimination; and from their halls
scores of young women are annually going
forth, thoroughly furnished for the domestic, industrial, educational, and religious
work of the world.

In devotion, effort, and sacrifice, our
women have at least equaled their brethren.

Benjamin Randall

In church development, church extension, and benevolent enterprises, they have efficiently served with their brethren on committees, councils, and boards.

For the aid of the churches in the support of missions at home and abroad, our women organized at General Conference held at Sutton, Vermont, in 1847. Since then their work has been both inspirational and executive. They instituted monthly meetings for prayer for missions and the dissemination of missionary intelligence. By "concerts," in which singing, recitations, and select readings were the order, they interested the children in missions. They raised, largely by self-sacrifice, money for the treasuries of all our benevolent operations.

Since 1874 the Woman's Missionary Society has constantly sustained missionaries in India, where they have established schools, a kindergarten hall, an orphanage, a widows' home, and a medical dispensary. Their missionaries have been especially successful as teachers, evangelists, and zenana workers.

True to its original purpose, the Woman's Missionary Society has sustained home as well as foreign missions, notably among the freedmen. From its treasury, college buildings have been erected, industrial departments have been instituted, and teachers sustained.

Though sustaining an independent treasury, the Woman's Society has not only maintained its own special work, but has, directly and indirectly, contributed thousands of dollars to parent boards, and has never closed its fiscal year in debt.

As to literature, the Woman's Society has created and distributed millions of pages of leaflets and booklets, and several standard works in more permanent form. Since 1878 it has published one of the neatest, sweetest, and ablest missionary magazines of our country, " The Missionary Helper."

After all, perhaps the most enduring work of "those women" has been of that quiet,

Benjamin Randall

instructive nature that has made possible the young people's movement, which, in turn, makes manifestation of itself in all manner of good work for humanity and for God, in all lands.

In monarchical countries, when the king or queen is "toasted," response is regarded as "bad form." It is claimed that the most brilliant encomiums would only cheapen royalty. Our sister is a daughter of the Great King. Laudation would only cheapen her royalty. It is enough that we point with honest pride to her character and her achievements—this we do—"*and let her own works praise her in the gates.*"

XL

BEGINNING with the example and precepts of Mr. Randall, our people have given special attention to the religious instruction of children and youth. Early in the last century they welcomed the Sunday-school as a cooperative factor. Since then, helped by an appropriate literature furnished by our publishing house, and receiving wise management from the church, the Sunday-school has grown to be a mighty power for good. Without diminishing in any way its own vigor or efficiency, the Sunday-school has evolved the young people's movement.

Mr. Harry S. Myers, A. M., a former professor in Hillsdale College, now a secretary of the Missionary Education Movement of the United States and Canada, and for several years general secretary of our de-

Benjamin Randall

nominational young people's organizations, in response to urgent request, kindly consented to write the record of our organized young people for this volume.

Had it not been for a suggestion of space limits, Secretary Myers would probably have included in this very excellent review more about the local work of our young people. In justice it should be said, however, that they contributed devotion to our meetings of worship, money to our treasuries, executive ability to administrative departments, and lifted our churches to broader planes of outlook and effort. For all this, much is due to the efficient supervision of former General Secretary Myers. His summary subjoined is both instructive and inspirational:

As long ago as the Civil War there was, in the Washington Street Free Baptist Church, at Dover, New Hampshire, an organization of young people for serious purposes, very similar to the plans which afterward developed into the general young

Benjamin Randall

people's societies. In 1876, in the Free Baptist church at Goblesville, Michigan, a young people's society was organized which has had a continuous existence until the present time. It was formed on exactly the same plan—with educational objects—as the Christian Endeavor Society, organized six years later, in Portland, Maine. As far as I know, this was the first real young people's society ever organized that really belongs to the modern young people's movement.

In 1886 the Free Baptists organized a denominational young people's society known as the Advocates of Christian Fidelity; and in 1888 this organization sent Rev. and Mrs. Edwin B. Stiles as missionaries to India, under the Free Baptist Foreign Mission Board. These were the first of a long list of many missionaries, who have gone to the foreign field, to be appointed by young people's organizations.

The name of the general organization was changed at the convention held at Fairport, New York, in 1897, to the United Society of Free Baptist Young People, and that name continued until May 26, 1912, when the organization ceased to exist as a

Benjamin Randall

separate entity, and was merged into the Young People's Department of the American Baptist Publication Society.

The young people's organization paid as large an amount as five thousand dollars two or three different years for missionary work outside of the local community, and had a total membership of thirteen thousand, which was the largest proportionate membership of any denominational young people's organization. And in the fall of 1907 there were more people in the Free Baptist churches engaged in mission study, proportionately, than in any other church. This was a result of the work carried on in connection with the young people's organization.

In 1911, with full authority of the General Conference of Free Baptists, it was voted by the Council of the United Society of Free Baptist Young People to unite the young people's work of the Free Baptists with the Baptists; and on Sunday afternoon, May 26, 1912, at the Northern Baptist Convention, in Des Moines, Iowa, I presented, amidst great enthusiasm, the gavel and block which had been the property of the United

Our "Sacred Mountain," produced the several woods which combine in this block and gavel. The oak grew so near the First New Durham Church that the voice of Benjamin Randall from its pulpit might have been echoed from the tree; the ash was taken from a tree that grew near Randall's grave; and the apple-wood came from the old parsonage orchard. This trinity not only suggests important historical facts, but may well represent the grandeur, the strength, and the fruitfulness of the United Society of Free Baptist Young People.

Made in the USA
Monee, IL
02 May 2021

67479916R00177